Misunderstood

Misunderstood is a relevant read, full of real life analogies, that helped me deepen my relationship with God. I went through the book with friends and enjoyed having both my eyes opened and my spirit stirred as we explored the character of God together. I love how each of the characteristics is accompanied by thought provoking questions to assist you in putting what you learned into immediate action!

—Robyn Beazley, Author of *Live An Amazing Life*, Motivational Speaker and Mompreneur

God longs to be known and understood. The same longing exists in the human heart. We crave connection that is safe and assumes the best of our motives, actions and thoughts. When we are misunderstood, it hurts. Yet we are quick to misjudge and question God's heart toward us. *Misunderstood* pulls back the curtain of confusion between man and God. Andrea shares eye-opening revelation and perspective on His unchanging, grace-filled nature that will eliminate misunderstanding and produce a deeper, more intimate trust in God. Our need for connection can only be satisfied as we believe in and experience the 'unfathomable, non-judgmental, absolutely immersing kind of love' that is found in the heart of God.

—Jan Greenwood, Author of *Women at War*, Equip Pastor, Gateway Church

As a person focused on exploring intimacy and relationship with Christ, I find myself more organically immersed in the literal Word of God and less in tangible studies designed to move readers through aspects of Christian faith. Knowing that, I was thrilled to discover the gifts of *Misunderstood*, a beautiful tool that works on so many levels of further knowing God. It allows the reader to blossom right where they are in their own journey of discovering who Jesus is through reference, explanation, and reflection. Whether a follower longing for more or a seeker getting a first glimpse of what is available through relationship, *Misunderstood* shatters what has held us back from the Truth of who we are and the profound love of a Father longing for His children to know His heart. Andrea's ability to communicate in such a personal and conversational manner, balanced with a non-threatening level of academic insight, draws readers into a place of relational exploration without distracting from the good and perfect Word of God. I have so many ideas on using this book, I cannot wait to share it!

—Amy Hauser, Author and Speaker, Made for More Ministries and Mosaics of Mercy

I have been blessed to study the Word of God with my friend, Andrea Moede. Her deep spiritual insights in *Misunderstood* flow out of her adventurous hunger for God and His truth. As she receives, she shares eagerly! Andrea's teaching stirs a witness in my heart, and I sense the power and anointing of the Holy Spirit. She inspires passion for fresh life and godliness in Christ. As a result, I am driven to shut out the enemy's distortion of who God is and grab the truth with a fierceness to live differently!

—Jeanne Rogers, Worship Leader and Ministry Representative, Life Today Television and Life Outreach International

As a community and youth worker, I minister on a daily basis with individuals who are in desperate need of healing and hope. I witness the reality of, where lies believed from a young age, manifest themselves in depression, addiction, abuse and brokenness in later life. *Misunderstood* has been an amazing resource in my professional practice, by helping me untangle some of these root-lies believed by those I work with and replacing them with God's truth. Whether ministering to inmates, youth or young single mothers, *Misunderstood* communicates so clearly the heart of God, our loving Father. As that is discovered, received and finally understood, it is a joy to witness identities, freedom and hope restored!

—Leah Westbrooks, Director of Community Development, 7More Ministries

We have used *Misunderstood* on different occasions for our women's ministry events. The new insights that the Holy Spirit gave our group while doing this study were an enormous blessing for all of the ladies involved. Personally, it gave me a fresh desire to get to know the character of God and pursue a daily, relevant relationship with Him, His Son, and the Holy Spirit. As Andrea so passionately communicates, the way we experience God is directly related to the way we view Him. This is why I believe this study is so vital for all believers, no matter how long they have been in church!

—Ashley Williams, Pastor and Missionary, First Anna Church

MISUNDERSTOOD

A Refreshing Guide To Dumping Religion For Good And Diving Deep Into A Personal Discovery Of The God Who Changes Everything

ANDREA JOY MOEDE

ISBN-13: 978-1-5214-9921-4
First Edition.

Published by The Fullness Thereof
P.O. Box 131342
Spring, Texas 77393

Editing by Brooke Copelin.
Cover design by Niezeka.
Formatting by Kindle_Format.

To receive your free bonus journal
that accompanies this book,
please visit us at

www.thefullnessthereof.com/bonusjournal

acknowledgements

To Him who is able to do immeasurably more than I could ask, think, or even imagine - thank you for creating me, loving me, pursuing me, and entrusting me with this piece of your heart. I hope I've made you proud.

Austen, Owen, Colsten, and Adelyn - thank you for giving of our family time together, so I could finally get this book into print. Your love and support are invaluable to me!

Ashley - for your ongoing encouragement and confidence in my teaching. Having your full support during those early days was an amazing boost for me.

Jeanne - for your unwavering help and cheering me on throughout the writing process. I know I would not have crossed the finish line without you.

And finally my sisters and soul-sisters near and far - thank you for your prayer coverage, listening ears, and deep friendships that give me an amazing place to be understood.

contents

Introduction – A Journey Begins

Can you imagine any greater pain than being misunderstood, particularly by those for whom you care most deeply? If we choose to admit it, this has happened to all of us at one time or another. I have quite a few circumstances I could list off at any given time! Whatever the situations were in your own life, I am sure you felt incredibly wounded in those moments. Whether justification ever comes is, in some ways, a moot point. You just want people to believe the best about you, and it hurts tremendously when they don't.

Imagine now if instead of just a handful of individuals misunderstanding you, it's actually in the millions or possibly even billions! I know I can't comprehend the scale of this, but it is what I believe God has constantly faced ever since He created mankind in the Garden of Eden and the enemy began his assault on us through an assault on what we believe about God.

Make no mistake that we do have an enemy (aka satan or the devil). He is the one deliberately creating shades of gray and making us doubt and misunderstand our creator God, who is actually defined by love and goodness. In fact, while the name satan means adversary or accuser, the word devil is defined as slanderer or one who maliciously tells lies about others. That should be a very revealing truth in regard to his primary battle strategy as he consistently lies to us about the character of our three-part God – our Heavenly Father, our Savior Jesus, and our Helper Holy Spirit.

[See John 8:44b - He was a murderer from the beginning, and does not stand in the truth, because there is no truth in him. When he lies, he speaks out of his own character, for he is a liar and the father of lies.]

The Bible is our guidebook and the only place we can go to counter the slander of God coming at us from every direction. This ancient text reveals that God has feelings and emotions just as we do, so it is a bit naïve to think He is completely above this pain of being misunderstood. So why would He not clear His name and set the record straight, especially considering the countless accusations leveled against Him every day?

The reason for His restraint lies deep at the root of why He created mankind in the first place. He wanted a family to lavish His love upon that would

16

choose to love and pursue Him in return, not a robotic people that would simply do as they were told. If the God of the universe (in all His glory) was consistently breaking in on us and defending Himself overtly, that wouldn't leave much room for our choice in the relationship, now would it?

An interesting picture of this is the contrast between a bride who has chosen the groom and one whose marriage has been arranged for her. A bride who has chosen knows the love of the man, has experienced his kindness and tenderness, and eagerly desires a life together. While a bride whose marriage has been arranged has merely been told to trust, based on the opinions of others, that this is the right decision. There is no tangible experience, no intimacy that encourages her onward, just a sense of duty that propels her into the match.

Do you think that God would really want to structure creation where all He gets in the end is an arranged-marriage bride, who will reluctantly drag herself to the altar? Of course not! He wants a people to choose Him above all else based on the ever-increasing weight of our love and connection. So yes, in a stunning move of humility and in honor of our free will to choose, He allows the misunderstandings surrounding His nature to occur.

As a result, God remains somewhat hidden for now, peeking out on occasion, beckoning us in to get to know Him, to come to believe the best about Him regardless of what we experience in this broken world. Yet very few choose to do so, most remaining back in the familiar spaces of religion. Regardless of your history with God, I hope that this book through the power of Holy Spirit awakens something in you to begin on this path. He is ever ready and willing to reveal Himself and correct all of our misunderstandings. In fact, there is nothing He would enjoy more; but we must take the time to sit and make room for His true personality to be revealed deep in our hearts.

The Bible also tells us that the more we observe and consider God, the more we will be transformed into His likeness. Seeing God and all that He is will not only correct our misconceptions and cause us to want to be closer to Him, it will also lead to our ultimate wholeness. Who doesn't want that!

[See II Corinthians 3:18 - And we all, with unveiled face, beholding the glory of the Lord, are being transformed into the same image from one

degree of glory to another. For this comes from the Lord who is the Spirit.]

As we move through time, there will be an ever-increasing unveiling of the heart of God, an adventure I believe will continue throughout eternity. Not only will all of our misunderstandings be erased, the things we do know about Him will continue to grow in magnitude and beauty. Exploration of Him will literally never end! This book is an attempt at relating what has been revealed to me so far, with the goal of whetting your appetite for more; and there will always and forever be more.

This is truly a journey and a fun one at that. So if you've never really explored God before, let's do this together – ten weeks spent ridding ourselves of stale religious ideas and instead discovering His true nature. You and I will never be the same.

Week 1 – Eternal & Unchanging

How do we even begin the topic of describing the God of the universe on a simple piece of paper with our limited words and understanding? It is a heady topic to be sure, but one we have all agreed is worth investigating. It says in the Bible that it is the glory of kings to search out a matter.

[See Proverbs 25:2 - It is the glory of God to conceal things, but the glory of kings is to search things out.]

How I want to be counted among the kings (and queens!) category; don't you? In this quest for searching out the concealed things of God, I encourage you to get your pens and highlighters out right now. This text is meant to be colored, underlined, and otherwise obnoxiously marked to highlight those things that God has to say to you specifically. Your return will be boosted greatly if you determine not to skim here but rather to digest. I will wait while you gather your supplies.

Right at the outset of our journey, it seems only natural to contemplate God's eternal and unchanging nature as one of the basic truths about Him presented in the Bible. Here are some definitions of these two attributes to get us going: Eternal is defined as existing forever, without end or beginning, valid for all time, endless, and essentially unchanging. Unchanging is defined as remaining the same and constant. Let's take a look at what a better understanding of this part of Him could mean for us and how we live our lives.

Fullness

In focusing on the eternal aspect of God, I don't think a timeline paradigm can begin to do it justice. Our finite minds simply cannot handle the idea of a 'line' that goes on without end. My husband, Austen, tells the story that he used to have trouble sleeping if he started thinking about eternity, granted this was at age five (deep thinker I know!). He says he would begin to think about this wind-up toy penguin he had, and it freaked him out to no end to think of the possibility of it going on forever and never stopping.

While a child certainly has trouble with the concept of an infinite timeline, adults can't truly comprehend it either. So instead, I attempt to think spatially, which I will admit is very difficult for my natural mind. I tend to be a very linear thinker (in my academic life, I was educated as a CPA). That should tell you all you need to know about how my brain works. I am sure a right-brained person could do this topic much better justice, but here goes.

What if we begin to think about God's eternalness as height, depth, width, and breadth of existence? That would bring whole different dimensions (literally) to what it means of the Godhead (Father, Son, and Holy Spirit). This spatial idea naturally leads to the concept of the fullness of God which is mentioned repeatedly throughout the Bible and has always been one of those topics that has grabbed my attention. Fullness is defined as completeness over a broad scope, the property of a sensation that is rich and pleasing, the condition of being filled to capacity, and greatness of volume.

If you think about it in this way, He actually surrounds everything that has ever been and ever will be. Wow! Can we even begin to imagine the immense space that would be required to house this richness? What might all of that area contain that we have never thought to attribute to Him before?

As we get to discussions of other attributes later, this idea of fullness will come into play. We don't just want an inkling of God's love – we want the fullness of it. We don't just want to touch the surface of how joyful He is – we want to experience all of it.

While discussing this idea of fullness may feel a bit nebulous, doesn't it almost make you hungry with expectation of the more of God that is available to those who will search Him out? Dare I say it? Until we are full? This topic of His eternal nature and His fullness tends to remind me that my spiritual appetite can really never be satisfied when I am honed in on Him, because it will just get richer and deeper as we go.

Constant

Turning now toward His unchanging nature, one of the definitions that was introduced earlier was that of being constant (something that does not or cannot change or vary). Now this is something my rule-following mind can grab hold of and process. I loved algebra when I was in high school; something about the orderliness of the subject just gets me. However, I did struggle with geometry, no doubt proving my lack of spatial capabilities discussed above!

In any case, in algebra the constant was always a comforting thing to see when staring down at the math problem. It was the known quantity, the one thing you could absolutely rely on to help you find the correct answer, and the very first place to start as you decided on your problem-solving strategy.

So now I wonder - do we consider our unchanging God in this same way, excited to see His presence in any given issue, knowing He is the constant that will help us reach the answer? Or do we sigh and look at Him as if He is the dreaded X or Y, the unknown quantity that baffles? Based on the way that many people speak about Him today, I would guess that the second statement would be more prevalent. Sadly, this often includes those who consider themselves believers in God.

It seems everywhere we turn, humanity just doesn't know what to expect from God anymore. In general, we don't trust Him when the going gets rough in this battle-weary world. So we huff and we puff and we bluff trying to make it on our own in a world of variables, all the while the unchanging constant is ever available if we would just trust Him. That, in short, is one of the main goals of this book: to help all of us believe that God is, at all times, the known quantity that we can rely on and approach first as we encounter the problems of life.

Security and Stability

The Bible says that God is eternal and unchanging – as I read these words now in combination, I think of the immense security this should imply in our lives. As natural parenting wisdom goes, it seems to be a largely universally held truth that one thing children need more than anything else are firm boundaries and steady people in their lives. Not that they could verbalize this desire, but that internal knowledge seems to be a part of their compass that is hard to replicate.

My husband and I have spent some time working with foster children, and this has to be the most noticeable difference between their mindset and that of children in other homes. They do not know (because they have not experienced) what it means to have someone in their life who does not move, no matter how things oscillate around them or how things shake not attached to them. The presence of such a person makes one secure in a very real sense of the word (secure - fixed or fastened so as not to give way, become loose, or be lost).

Obviously as human parents, we do not have the eternal characteristic of God; but just the part of being unchanging can do something tremendous for how safe and secure a child feels, and by extension, how they act. Now multiply that exponentially when you add in the factor that not only is our Father God perfectly unchanging (as we could only hope to be), He is also that way for all of time.

This is who we have loving us, supporting us, and cheering us on when we choose to believe in the God of the Bible – He is the ultimate standard in secure living for all of us in His family. When we begin to understand this, we should never have to return to those unbelievably low places of wallowing in doubt, fear, and anxiety (all signs of insecurity). We should actually be the most confident people in the world, because we are attached to the most secure One in existence.

Another way of thinking about these two attributes together would be to realize the stability we should have even in very unsteady times. While I don't have experience sailing, I have taken flying lessons; and one thing that I learned was the value of the horizon. When navigating with instruments by air or when trying to regain your footing on sea, finding the horizon (the line at which the earth's surface and sky appear to meet) and setting your eyes on it can be of great assistance. This is because the horizon stretches on indefinitely (eternal) in both directions, providing a fixed (unchanging) line on which to focus, even while your body might in fact be pitching up and down.

How often in life do we feel as if we are not standing on solid ground, when the circumstances of this broken world send us reeling, even to the point of getting off course or losing our lunch? God can be our horizon; He is fully equipped by his eternal and unchanging nature to be that stabilizing line in our lives. But we cannot continue to look down at where our feet should be and expect this capability of His to be of any use. Instead, we must look up to find and focus on Him.

Wrapping Up

So what in this discussion has grabbed your attention? What part of God have you misunderstood regarding His eternal and unchanging nature? Or should I say, what part has the enemy been determined to keep you blinded to? Often, it is the very thing the enemy attacks most in our individual lives that gives us a clue to our destiny of who God has called us to be, so let's all pay close attention to these areas.

We do tend to have our candy-coated, perfectly ideal, maybe even Sunday-school ideas of God etched in our minds. Yes of course, we say we believe that He is eternal and unchanging; but has this truth really been cemented in our hearts? I believe the best way to answer that question is to consider how we are living right now, which is ultimately a reflection of what we believe about Him. Full or Empty? Constant or Variable? Secure or Insecure? Stable or Unstable?

If you find these probing questions a little uncomfortable, that's good; so do I. Maybe we all need a little Ready-Mix to help cement the true reality of these attributes deep inside of us. Let's allow the help of Holy Spirit to fill in these gaps in our understanding as we focus on God's eternal and unchanging nature this week. May we all grow and experience Him in new ways as we do so!

Week 1 Reflections and Meditations

Reflect: Think back to a time when you felt alone and misunderstood. Can you list a few adjectives as to how that situation affected you? In that moment, what would have provided the most healing for your heart?

Meditate: Glance through the Week 1 Scriptures and pick several to meditate on this week. Write them in the space below, make a notecard, or create a memo on your phone to keep them handy. Writing them helps, speaking them helps, and praying them to God helps most of all.

Apply: As you go through this week, be aware of the times when you slip into doubt, fear, anxiety, or insecurity. Check yourself as you picture and believe that He is the security and stability of your life, so those feelings lose their place. Journal the details below.

Week 1 Scripture Listing

Fullness

Psalm 16:11 - You make known to me the path of life; in your presence there is fullness of joy; at your right hand are pleasures forevermore.

Psalm 24:1 - The earth is the LORD's and the fullness thereof, the world and those who dwell therein.

John 1:16 - For from his fullness we have all received, grace upon grace.

Romans 15:29 - I know that when I come to you I will come in the fullness of the blessing of Christ.

Ephesians 3:17-19 - So that Christ may dwell in your hearts through faith—that you, being rooted and grounded in love, may have strength to comprehend with all the saints what is the breadth and length and height and depth, and to know the love of Christ that surpasses knowledge, that you may be filled with all the fullness of God.

Constant

Numbers 23:19 - God is not man, that he should lie, or a son of man, that he should change his mind. Has he said, and will he not do it? Or has he spoken, and will he not fulfill it?

Malachi 3:6 - For I the Lord do not change; therefore you, O children of Jacob, are not consumed.

Hebrews 13:8 - Jesus Christ is the same yesterday and today and forever.

James 1:17 - Every good gift and every perfect gift is from above, coming down from the Father of lights with whom there is no variation or shadow due to change.

Security & Stability

Psalm 40:2 - He drew me up from the pit of destruction, out of the miry bog, and set my feet upon a rock, making my steps secure.

Psalm 62:2 - He only is my rock and my salvation, my fortress; I shall not be greatly shaken.

Psalm 93:2 - Your throne is established from of old; you are from everlasting.

Psalm 102:12 - But you, O LORD, are enthroned forever; you are remembered throughout all generations.

II Samuel 22:32 - For who is God, but the Lord? And who is a rock, except our God?

Isaiah 26:4 - Trust in the Lord forever, for the Lord God is an everlasting rock.

Isaiah 33:6a - And He will be the stability of your times, abundance of salvation, wisdom, and knowledge.

John 8:58 - Jesus said to them, "Truly, truly, I say to you, before Abraham was, I am."

Hebrews 6:19 - We have this as a sure and steadfast anchor of the soul, a hope that enters into the inner place behind the curtain.

Revelation 1:8 - "I am the Alpha and the Omega," says the Lord God, "who is and who was and who is to come, the Almighty."

Week 2 – All-Powerful, Knowing & Present

So how did you do last week on the reflections and meditations? Was it difficult to sit quietly at first? Did you find it became easier and perhaps more refreshing as the week continued? I know for an active person like myself, learning to spend time in contemplative, listening prayer was very difficult in the beginning; but once I began, I could not get enough. It has become a highlight of my day – to steal away for as many moments as I can to just rest and listen – that is until my kids find my hiding place.

To begin, it may help to set up a specific place with a few tangible things to motivate you, such as a comfortable chair, a few pillows, a cup of coffee or tea, maybe even some good music. I can confidently promise that the more you make a habit of this and enjoy His tangible presence, the less you will need these physical things to get you there. You can also pray that God will help draw you when your motivation lags.

[See Song of Solomon 1:4a - Draw me after you; let us run.]

As we embark this week, I look at the attributes above and again ponder where to begin with such a vast topic, while also knowing that Holy Spirit will have some fantastic things to reveal here. These are all of the omni-'s of God that you may have heard: omnipotent (all-powerful), omniscient (all-knowing), and omnipresent (all-present). This list has always sounded so religious to me but has never held a great deal of meaning. Here's to pulling the shroud off of them and bringing their power into our everyday lives.

The prefix 'omni-' simply means all or every. 'Potent' is defined as having great power, influence, or effect. 'Scient' involves that which is knowing or skillful. And finally, 'present' describes being or existing at this time or now. Let's move on to some applications of these attributes.

All-Powerful

Few people would argue with this attribute of God in general. It is the very thing that sets Him apart from us as the supreme being. So while most agree that He is all-powerful, we have the emphasis all wrong. We tend to focus (even if it is subconsciously) on the domination or control that this characteristic could mean, which then brings up ideas of dictators or superheroes or maybe some of both. To test my theory, ask yourself: what image popped into my mind when I read the title all-powerful? Yes, He spoke the universe into existence. And yes, He can do anything. But there is so much more to it than that, and I believe that we have neglected the myriad of other ways His power is displayed.

For starters, there is the fact that He gave us a free will, as we discussed in the introduction of this book. He created people in order to have a larger family to share His life and love with and then gave us the power to choose whether to have a relationship with Him. This not only surrendered what He could have dominated (our choice), but it also opened Him up to a world of hurt.

[See Hosea 11:8b - My heart is torn within me, and my compassion overflows.]

So He regularly stands by, allowing the very people to whom He is giving every breath to despise and reject Him. Can you imagine? This is not just raw power as we might have imagined, charging forward like a pack of wild horses frothy with sweat. This is tremendous power under restraint (bound by the integrity of His own word), which I would venture to say is the greatest power of all.

Another show of His power is in His delegation of authority over the earth to mankind. When He created Adam and Eve in the beginning, He instructed them to fill, govern, and reign over the earth (See Genesis 1:28). This authority was handed over to satan when they sinned, and the earth came under his control. Even then, God restrained His power, abided by His Word, and put a plan into place to redeem the authority of man. This was accomplished by sending His son, Jesus, to live and die as a human being (See John 3:16-17). When this willing sacrifice submitted to the law of death, having committed no sin, the evil system was forever broken down and satan was disarmed (See Colossians 2:15). This brought the authority over the earth back to where God had placed it, into the hands of man (See Psalm 115:16).

All of that to say, in my business career, I observed many people who appeared to have power, but it was not absolute. God is not like a middle-manager who pretends to delegate authority and then takes it back when things are not going well; that is not releasing your power at all – it's merely pretense. He also is not like an executive that delegates power, only to get in trouble with the board of directors or stockholders for poor decisions by his managers. He is actually more like the owner and sole equity holder, and His power is backed up by no other. Only one with the final say of authority can make such a bold decision as to give some of the power away, and then stick with it, regardless of the results.

Now this last application may stretch you a little bit, as it did me, but where's the fun in not taking some risks? As mentioned earlier, potent's dictionary definition is having great power, influence, or effect. When I first glanced at the word though, my mind quickly raced through terms that had this root word, and I came up with...impotent. This term essentially means a male who is unable to produce life. It is quite a stigma for any man to be associated with this word, much less God. Yet how often do we not account for His life-giving ability and regard Him as impotent? Ouch, I know that one hurt. We may not say as much, but our actions and attitudes reveal otherwise. When in actuality, not only is He potent, but He is omni-potent or containing all and every ability to produce life in any situation. Let's stretch ourselves with that next 'impossible' situation in our lives and believe for God's omnipotence to come into play.

As we wind down this attribute, I want to challenge you with a new image to replace the one that may have popped up at the beginning of the section.

Instead of an over-arching or heavy-handed idea of God as the all-powerful One, what if it becomes a gracious and ultimately open-handed one instead? His is the kind of power that gives and does not take.

All-Knowing

If you are a thinker or analyzer in any way, then I am sure you have bumped up against this attribute of God. I will be the first to admit that I have as well. If ever there was a person capable of thinking something to death, that would be me. As a culture, we have progressed to the point of being addicted to logic and reasoning. Intellectual capability is fine, until it removes the place of faith and trust in God that is so pivotal to having an over-coming life.

Even among believers, we spend a lot of time analyzing decision points and pro's and con's lists. It does not appear to be a huge affront to God to try to plan your way and make the best choices; but I have come to see that it is actually one of the most subtle forms of self-occupation, which elevates our human knowledge and wisdom.

[See Proverbs 14:12 - There is a path before each person that seems right, but it ends in death.]

This Scripture reveals what will happen if we insist on charting our own way according to our knowledge and what seems right in our minds – the death of goals, dreams, and maybe even life itself. So what are we to do? The Bible says that we should be like children in our faith.

[See Luke 18:17 - I tell you the truth, anyone who doesn't receive the Kingdom of God like a child will never enter it.]

So what does this mean practically? I asked our five year-old as a test case why he thought God knows way more than we do. His response? 'Because He is bigger and stronger and created the whole world. Those are really good reasons, and I am sure an adult off-the-cuff answer would be similar. However, when trying circumstances arise and we are less focused on God, how do we actually act? Our son gave a great answer in that moment, but I also remember the times that he certainly thought and acted as if he knew better than his parents. We have all done the same with God.

I believe the only way then to lay aside our logic (regardless of age) and trust that God knows best is through our increased awareness and personal experience of Him. Asking Him what He thinks, being patient enough to wait and listen, implementing only what He says to do, and seeing the incredible results that could not have happened any other way – these are the foundation stones of truly living a life trusting in His character. Experiences such as these are what build our faith in His all-knowing nature and in revealing how small our lens actually was on any given situation.

It will not be easy to lay down the constant analyzing and assessing, especially if this has become a regular habit. However once accomplished, it will lead to more peace and much better decisions. As we endeavor to make this change, the healthiest thing we can ask for are breadcrumbs: picking up bite-size pieces of information along the way, that keep us going in the right direction, while not getting ahead of God, and also keeping us motivated in pursuit.

I do understand that some people have more of a bent in an analytical direction, due to temperament and gifting from God. This attribute will be more of a struggle for them, but they also have such enormous potential on the up-side once they do receive this revelation. God created our human intellect for a reason, to do amazing things for Him; but just like anything else, it must be submitted for it to have its full effect.

I keep picturing a funnel as I think of this. Say you are a highly gifted individual and your 'funnel' has all of the right attributes in the natural to be the best of its kind: its top is very wide, its internal surface is smooth and slippery, while the outside has just the right grip, and the bottom is the perfect size to fit most receptors. With what speed and fluidity could God pour His all-knowingness through such a funnel? But what mess might this make if the funnel did not cooperate in the hands of the maker? I want to encourage you to spend time this week dwelling on this part of God. As we see Him in His sufficiency – may we become humble, submitted, shockingly good funnels of His knowledge into the world.

All-Present

The last attribute of being all-present seems more difficult to comprehend at face-value than the others. So this God that we speak of is everywhere all of the time? I don't know about you, but that is enough to make my brain explode if I stay there too long. While this is the traditional view of being present, I came across an alternate definition that grabbed my attention: that part of eternity dividing the domain of disappointment from the realm of hope. Now while I certainly don't think everything that lies in the past should be viewed as a disappointment – this definition did seem to offer a very real sense of the tension involved between the past and the future – or the present in which we all live. It is the space in which we make our choices.

[See Philippians 3:13-14 - Brothers, I do not consider that I have made it my own. But one thing I do: forgetting what lies behind and straining forward to what lies ahead, I press on toward the goal for the prize of the upward call of God in Christ Jesus.]

This is a conscious decision that every human being must make daily. Whether it has any spiritual component or not, will we be able to leave the past behind and move forward into the future? In fact, it is in this place where depression resides and actually keeps people firmly in its clutches. For various reasons, they are not able to break out of the tension and press forward toward any goal at all. Some combination of what has happened and what might come has rendered them hopeless and motionless. Even if you are not embroiled in a battle with depression right now, that attitude is always right there at the door, ready to take advantage of any opportunity to make your mind head in that direction.

This is where we all need a divine touch from God; for as we believe, He is omnipresent, therefore living outside of this tension. Only someone from His perspective, who sees the end from the beginning and lives outside of time, can absolutely assure us that there is hope for the future.

[See Isaiah 46:10 - Declaring the end from the beginning and from ancient times things not yet done, saying, 'My counsel shall stand, and I will accomplish all my purpose.']

Other people can attempt to comfort and console us when we are in trouble, but they will just be providing those soothing coping mechanisms – comfort and consolation. Only time spent with the all-present, almighty God will restore our fortitude in the ever-changing present and keep us moving forward in hope.

Putting It All Together

This chapter is a cheese-grater on our pride to be sure. After all, we are pointing out and dwelling on the fact that God contains the entire scope of these important attributes, which by default, means we have a lot less of them if we are being honest with ourselves. However, and this is a big contrasting conjunction, the sooner we realize and acknowledge this, the sooner we can begin to partner with Him and draw from His inexhaustible supply.

That means that you can be tapped into the power, knowledge, and presence of God as you walk through this life. He is not going to hand out these gifts and revelations though to people who have not laid down their pride and egos and acknowledged that He is the ultimate source from where all of their success flows.

[See James 4:6b - Therefore it says, "God opposes the proud, but gives grace to the humble."]

I remember a conversation I had a few years ago with a family member who is around my same age. She was impressed with the accomplishments our little family had achieved, and I just kept redirecting the praise to God. After a few of these comments and rebuttals, she said exasperatingly, 'Well, you have to take some credit for yourself.' While I understood her point of view, I also knew it was God who had created me, gifted me, and drawn me to His heart. I really was not being self-effacing, just transparent and honest with where I knew the success had come from. Of course, this attitude was a far cry from the eighteen year-old know-it-all who had once written a line at the end of high school that read, 'Do it yourself.' It was in that moment of stark contrast that I had to laugh as I realized the progress made. This progression did not happen through some big, intentional effort. Rather it was simply through time spent over the years listening to and growing in Him.

So while I know that pride is certainly an ugly thing, I don't believe it is as hard to overcome as some may suppose. When we begin to ponder and try to fathom who God really is, it becomes quite easy to step back and realize how little we truly are. And to further realize, how amazingly blessed we are to be created, loved, and elevated by this fully complete God into partnership with Him. Most of the time, the lack of this revelation of His grandness and our smallness (and thus our resulting pride) is because we have not yet taken adequate time to be still in His presence.

[See Psalm 46:10 - Be still, and know that I am God. I will be exalted among the nations, I will be exalted in the earth!]

Whether it is busyness, spiritual boredom, worldliness, or other factors – this distraction from time in His presence is one of the enemy's greatest tools in keeping us from hearing and seeing God. Once we do begin to brush away the cobwebs and put

Him as the primary focus in our lives, He will begin to reveal Himself to us. Our pride will naturally begin melting away as we behold His all. Let's have a great week purposing in our hearts to see more clearly our all-powerful, all-knowing, and all-present God.

Week 2 Reflections & Meditations

Reflect: Try to remember a situation in your life when you felt powerless, needing wisdom and perspective. Now reframe that circumstance with someone by your side who could provide all of what you needed. What might have changed as a result?

Meditate: Glance through the Week 2 Scriptures and pick several to meditate on this week. Write them in the space below, make a notecard, or create a memo on your phone to keep them handy. Writing them helps, speaking them helps, and praying them to God helps most of all.

Apply: Be purposeful this week in paying attention to situations where your lack and need are evident and on display. Instead of resenting them, grasp these moments as a perfect time to rest and lean in to His all. Journal the details below.

Week 2 Scripture Listing

All-Powerful

-Job 26:13-14 - By his wind the heavens were made fair; his hand pierced the fleeing serpent. Behold, these are but the outskirts of his ways, and how small a whisper do we hear of him! But the thunder of his power who can understand?"

-Psalm 62:11-12a - Once God has spoken; twice have I heard this: that power belongs to God, and that to you, O Lord, belongs steadfast love.

-Psalm 115:16 - The heavens are the LORD's heavens, but the earth he has given to the children of man.

-Jeremiah 10:12 - It is he who made the earth by his power, who established the world by his wisdom, and by his understanding stretched out the heavens.

-Zephaniah 3:17 - The LORD your God is in your midst, a mighty one who will save; he will rejoice over you with gladness; he will quiet you by his love; he will exult over you with loud singing.

-John 1:4 - In him was life, and the life was the light of men.

-I Corinthians 6:14 - And God raised the Lord and will also raise us up by his power.

-Colossians 1:28-29 - Him we proclaim, warning everyone and teaching everyone with all wisdom, that we may present everyone mature in Christ. For this I toil, struggling with all his energy that he powerfully works within me.

All-Knowing

-Job 37:16 - Do you know the balancing of the clouds, the wondrous works of him who is perfect in knowledge?

-Psalm 139:6 - Such knowledge is too wonderful for me; it is high; I cannot attain it.

-Psalm 147:5-6 - Great is our Lord, and abundant in power; his understanding is beyond measure. The LORD lifts up the humble; he casts the wicked to the ground.

-Isaiah 55:8-9 - For my thoughts are not your thoughts, neither are your ways my ways, declares the LORD. For as the heavens are higher than the earth, so are my ways higher than your ways and my thoughts than your thoughts.

-I John 3:19-20 - By this we shall know that we are of the truth and reassure our heart before him; for whenever our heart condemns us, God is greater than our heart, and he knows everything.

All-Present

-Job 28:24 - For he looks to the ends of the earth and sees everything under the heavens.

-Isaiah 46:9-10 - For I am God, and there is no other; I am God, and there is none like me, declaring the end from the beginning and from ancient times things not yet done.

-Jeremiah 23:23-24 - Am I a God at hand, declares the LORD, and not a God far away? Can a man hide himself in secret places so that I cannot see him? declares the LORD. Do I not fill heaven and earth? declares the LORD.

-Matthew 28:20 - And behold, I am with you always, to the end of the age.

-Acts 17:27-28 – That they should seek God, and perhaps feel their way toward him and find him. Yet he is actually not far from each one of us, for "In him we live and move and have our being."

-Colossians 1:17 - And he is before all things, and in him all things hold together.

Week 3 – Sovereign and Just

As we are moving through the weeks, it is so important to take our temperature and gauge our progress. This can help in staying motivated and drawing more from the weeks ahead, as we build layer upon layer of fresh insight. So how has your image of God changed over the last two weeks? I tend to visualize the process of receiving from God as going through each person's individual filter of their image of God. Just as a water filter can have an enormous impact on the flavor of the resulting water, how we each see God can drastically color or flavor even those special and unique revelations that Holy Spirit imparts.

Recently I was talking to a friend that has been walking with God for several decades longer than I have, and she said something so simple that struck me: 'You know, it just gets sweeter as you go.' And then I began to think, what will our relationship with Him 'taste' like once we have finished our earthly race, actually seen a glimpse of His glory, and are heading off into eternity?

[See Psalm 119:103 - How sweet are your words to my taste, sweeter than honey to my mouth!]

In light of this, do you feel your personal view of God has changed for the better? Do you feel as if your filter has become clearer and that you can receive more purely from Him as a result? Even in writing these pages, God has been reminding me of the truth of His attributes as I have encountered and moved through various life circumstances. This process has been giving my mind and spirit more good to grab onto and believe, rather than what surrounds me in the world. I hope that your time spent in quiet, as well as the time spent in the regular rhythm of your day, have begun to taste sweeter as together we refute the enemy's defamation of God's character.

[See Philippians 4:8 - Finally, brothers, whatever is true, whatever is honorable, whatever is just, whatever is pure, whatever is lovely, whatever is commendable, if there is any excellence, if there is anything worthy of praise, think about these things.]

Sovereign

Traditionally, the word sovereign has related to royalty of some sort – either a king, queen, or other supreme ruler. It also carries with it the idea of government and preeminence. An interesting aside to these typical definitions are the additional implications the word has for the authority that is being described. If you study the term historically and politically, it places an almost moral requirement on the entity that is exercising the sovereignty. Said another way, to be sovereign is to have the ability to guarantee the best interests of those being ruled, to the point of it being a moral obligation. If the authority is not consistently representing the best interests of its constituents, then it cannot be called a sovereign state – another type of government maybe, but not sovereign.

Typically in religious circles though, the attribute of the sovereignty of God has been sadly distorted. Teachers and preachers alike have used it as the scapegoat word to say that God can do whatever He wants – as in to heal or not to heal, to provide or not to provide, etc. This kind of teaching means well in trying to communicate the absolute preeminence and supremeness of God which I am not questioning. However, in doing so, it shortchanges such an important part of the attribute – that of Him always having the ability to guarantee our best interests.

When we accept Jesus and choose to come into the sovereign Kingdom of God, we become citizens under this type of authority. Yes, He is the ultimate ruler; but He will act in consistency with His nature, as revealed in the Bible. He is not some inconsistent renegade. He will not do things for us necessarily, but He will set up a structure facilitating our success if we do our part. This is what you would expect from any natural sovereign state, and we should expect no less from the Kingdom of Heaven.

[See Philippians 3:20 (AMP) - But we are citizens of the state (commonwealth, homeland) which is in heaven, and from it also we earnestly and patiently await [the coming of] the Lord Jesus Christ (the Messiah) [as] Savior.]

The reason I use the word scapegoat to describe the teaching above is that it seems these religious minds cannot cope with all of the brokenness of the world. They have struggled to find a way out for God, and in reality, a way out for themselves. Not able to answer the perplexing questions about hardship and suffering, they have created a theology that says, 'Well that's just God, and He can do whatever He wants, even if we don't understand.' In my limited experience, this is generally what begins to be taught when someone mentions the sovereignty of God. You can also expect a deep throat gurgle to be thrown in for emphasis!

Now I cannot explain suffering any better, but I do know that we are in the middle of an all-out warzone and that God has delegated authority over the earth to man. Sometimes, even when we have done all we know to do, the perfect Biblical results still do not manifest. We obviously do not have all the answers yet; but I believe God is looking for people who will contend for His best according to the promises in the Word, no matter what we actually see. When we do take this stand, God will then release revelation about why certain problems have not yet submitted to the name of Jesus, which we know eventually they all must do.

[See Philippians 2:9-11 - Therefore God has highly exalted him and bestowed on him the name that is above every name, so that at the name of Jesus every knee should bow, in heaven and on earth and under the earth, and every tongue confess that Jesus Christ is Lord, to the glory of God the Father.]

Unfortunately, the twisting of this attribute of God has been powerful in the hands of the enemy, even if it is to barely get his foot in the door and make us start questioning if God is truly looking out for our best interests. We have to uproot any trace of that seed being sown into the soil of our hearts. I do find it intriguing that the natural world has such a clear understanding of this attribute, while spiritually we struggle and debate it.

Today, let us refuse to allow what we see or do not see to change our perception of His absolute sovereignty as the King over the Kingdom of Heaven. We must know that He is setting all of us up to succeed by looking out for our best interests. Let us also believe that by closing this door of opportunity to the enemy, our sovereign God will speak ever clearly to us about how He would have us conquer the difficult and seemingly insurmountable obstacles of our day.

Just

What is your first thought when you consider that the Bible states that God is just and that He consistently brings justice? Did the word 'fair' come to mind? It did for me. The two words are listed as synonyms, but there is a slight difference. See if you can spot it in the definitions that follow: just - guided by truth, correct, equitable; fair - in accordance with rules or standards, legitimate.

It appears that while just is being held to the ultimate standard of truth, fair is being held to established rules or standards. There is a difference in the level of authority to which the appeal is being made. Depending on the circumstances then, a person or decision that is fair must relate to a smaller arena where rules have been established (such as a school or governmental system). While a person or decision that is just is relating to a larger realm of being truthful or absolutely correct. Is it any wonder then that God is described in Scripture as being just rather than fair? He actually is the larger realm and the standard of ultimate truth and correctness.

So have you ever wondered why people crave justice and react so strongly when it is violated? We have all seen when someone totally flips out (think road rage or waiting in line). These explosive reactions always seem to be rooted in some perceived breach of justice. I believe this is because we are made in the image of God, and this part of His character (justice) is embedded in us. We just haven't quite figured out how to handle it.

[See Genesis 1:27 - So God created man in his own image, in the image of God he created him; male and female he created them.]

This goes for the most devout believer to the most staunch atheist. Deep in all human beings, there seems to be this universal idea of a supreme standard of right and wrong (which I believe emanates from God) that causes a passionate response if circumstances contradict it. As I have observed such deep emotional reactions by people to unfair situations, it occurred to me that He must feel just as strongly as we do about it. For Him, how much greater must these feelings be as He watches His once-perfect creation, now fractured by sin, continue to destroy itself?

Yet, God continues to abide by His word and work through people on the earth. If I were in his shoes, I think I might disregard what I had promised, swing in to save the day, and stop whatever injustice was occurring. While that is what a lot of us hope for (and then shake our fists at God when He does not intervene), it would have terrible results. It would absolutely undermine our trust in Him and His Word. There is great comfort to me in knowing that while He is just and will facilitate the implementation of His justice (including working through us), He does not break the integrity of His word. He stands by His giving authority over the earth to man, even when everyone's emotions are screaming. Do you know what this really means for us? We can take everything written in the Bible and know that He is bound to it, even when it's breaking His heart.

As I was writing the section above looking at the word 'just' as an adjective, I also began thinking about it as an adverb. It is used often in this second way as a qualifier meaning 'merely.' For example: I am just saying or I just want to know. Even though it is operating as a different part of speech, this is a pretty marked departure from the earlier definitions. So when describing a thing, just means truth; but when describing an action, it means merely. It seems like the requested action is for justice but with a weak will, with the possibility of it going either way, instead of confidently knowing that we have a just judge presiding over all.

I wonder if this shift in the meaning of our word happened over time, as people have become more and more numb to the darkness of the world and the manifestations of less than God's best? We have lost confidence and are living in a 'merely' realm. I do understand this is due in large part because we have not always seen His justice manifest, but I contend that this is not His fault. We are instruments of His justice here – whether it is financially providing the funds to feed people that are starving to death, praying for the healing miracle in the person's body being destroyed by sickness from the enemy, or being a solid reference for the person that lost their employment. He is doing His part and giving us the provision (whether it is financial, powerful, or directional) to partner with Him in bringing justice to a broken world. Are we doing ours?

Another interesting part of this discussion is your personal idea of what justice or fairness look like. Often, when people say these terms, they really mean equal. When kids yell or grown adults complain, 'That's not fair,' they are not really contending for justice or fairness. They are pleading for equality. However, equality is not part of the definition, but equitableness is. Equal means to divide into the same size, while equitable means to divide fairly. All of us have very different paths to walk, and God will ensure that we receive justice individually. However, it may not look like what He does for others, and therein lies our problem. When we have had to combat illness, spend time in the unemployment lines, or deal with wayward children, it can be frustrating to see others who appear to be blessed in every area.

We have bought into the mindset of the world (which is really agreeing with the enemy's lies) that says we should all be treated the same, instead of relying on Holy Spirit to be our individual compass and trusting God's character in every situation. If some attack has prevailed and you know that God's best has not yet manifested in your life, take a step back and pause for a moment. Instead of looking around and comparing, begin asking what His justice will look like for you in that situation. He is working to bring things back around on your behalf. So do not let your eyes rest on others, but rather hone in on His promises.

As a final note on this attribute, we have all seen situations that were not resolved to God's standard of justice here on earth. So I will leave you with this great promise for full resolution in eternity.

[See Revelation 21:1-7 - Then I saw a new heaven and a new earth, for the first heaven and the first earth had passed away, and the sea was no more. And I saw the holy city, new Jerusalem, coming down out of heaven from God, prepared as a bride adorned for her husband. And I heard a loud voice from the throne saying, "Behold, the dwelling place of God is with man. He will dwell with them, and they will be his people, and God himself will be with them as their God. He will wipe away every tear from their eyes, and death shall be no more, neither shall there be

mourning, nor crying, nor pain anymore, for the former things have passed away. "And he who was seated on the throne said, "Behold, I am making all things new." Also he said, "Write this down, for these words are trustworthy and true." And he said to me, "It is done! I am the Alpha and the Omega, the beginning and the end. To the thirsty I will give from the spring of the water of life without payment. The one who conquers will have this heritage, and I will be his God and he will be my son."]

Final Exam

As we close out this week, think about where you have seen God's hands at work and His divine orchestration operating in the symphony of your life. If nothing is prompted, I encourage you to ask Him to show you where His sovereignty and justice have prevailed, even if you did not know it at the time. Only very recently did Holy Spirit reveal such a circumstance to me that occurred in my childhood.

My family and I recently moved back to my hometown upon a sudden job promotion. I never anticipated that I would be back in this geographic area, but God has been using the change to reveal many things. He directed us to a church that is now led by former youth pastors of my older siblings. I did not consciously think I had much of a connection to them, as I was a young child when we were part of that church. That is, until Holy Spirit said a few simple words: 'They were sheltering her as she was sheltering you.'

As I heard these words, I saw levels of cascading umbrellas. I began to see that during that tumultuous time in our family that involved severe mental illness battles, God had set up a structure of protection for this then six year-old. My older sister was instrumental in protecting the younger kids from a lot of what was going on, and we have thanked her for that in recent years; but never before had I seen the others involved. It was as if these young youth pastors, who had no idea what they were doing at the time, were placed there by God to cover my sister. In doing this, they were another level of covering, shielding the rest of us from the spiritual shrapnel that was flying, which could have wounded us...even fatally so.

Upon this revelation, I wrote them a letter, wanting them to know their impact and thanking them for those seeds that were sown. As I proof-read the letter, I just doubled over on the floor in awe of the sovereignty and justice of God, completely unbeknownst to me for the last twenty-five years. It hit me afresh and anew that He is always seeing, always moving, always protecting through amazing, submitted vessels such as these. And how many others were there or have there been that I still have not had the privilege of seeing?

Was any of that situation intended by the sovereignty of God? Would any of that situation have stood firm in His court of justice? The answer to both of those questions is a resounding no. It was an ugly, enemy-initiated scheme to destroy many lives – but for the character of God. He provided just the right ingredients to look out for all of our best interests and correct those circumstances into something that lined up with His ultimate truth in our lives.

I wish I could come through these pages to sit and pray with you to hear some of your own orchestration tale. Just as a symphony is a long piece of music with many movements, these stories often play out over a lifetime; so do not be surprised if you feel as if you have only seen a glimpse. Keep at it though; these encounters are the ones that mark you forever and draw you so close to His side. Wait, wait, wait on God this week and as you do, may you hear your own unique and intriguing story straight from the heart of our sovereign and just Father.

Week 3 Reflections & Meditations

Reflect: In your life history with God, have there been moments when you believed that He was the one who caused suffering? What about times when you specified the way you thought His justice should intervene? If yes, what was your resulting emotional state and spiritual atmosphere from those thought processes?

Meditate: Glance through the Week 3 Scriptures and pick several to meditate on this week. Write them in the space below, make a notecard, or create a memo on your phone to keep them handy. Writing them helps, speaking them helps, and praying them to God helps most of all.

Apply: Practice living in the Kingdom of Heaven. Consider as you walk out your door this week that you have a King who is looking out for your best interests and a Judge who will ensure that truth will prevail. How is your stature, mood, and countenance as you do so? Journal the details below.

Week 3 Scripture Listing

Sovereign

-I Chronicles 29:11-12 - Yours, O Lord, is the greatness and the power and the glory and the victory and the majesty, for all that is in the heavens and in the earth is yours. Yours is the kingdom, O Lord, and you are exalted as head above all. Both riches and honor come from you, and you rule over all. In your hand are power and might, and in your hand it is to make great and to give strength to all.

-Psalm 103:19 - The Lord has established his throne in the heavens, and his kingdom (sovereignty) rules over all.

-Proverbs 19:21 - Many are the plans in the mind of a man, but it is the purpose of the LORD that will stand.

-Isaiah 48:17 - Thus says the LORD, your Redeemer, the Holy One of Israel: "I am the LORD your God, who teaches you to profit, who leads you in the way you should go."

-Romans 8:28 - And we know that for those who love God all things work together for good, for those who are called according to his purpose.

-Philippians 2:13 - For it is God who works in you, both to will and to work for his good pleasure.

-Hebrews 2:9 - But we see him who for a little while was made lower than the angels, namely Jesus, crowned with glory and honor because of the suffering of death, so that by the grace of God he might taste death for everyone.

Just

-Deuteronomy 32:4 – The Rock, his work is perfect, for all his ways are justice.   A God of faithfulness and without iniquity, just and upright is he.

-Job 37:23 - The Almighty—we cannot find him; he is great in power; justice and abundant righteousness he will not violate.

-Isaiah 43:2 – When you pass through the waters, I will be with you; and through the rivers, they shall not overwhelm you; when you walk through fire you shall not be burned, and the flame shall not consume you.

-Psalm 33:5 - He loves righteousness and justice; the earth is full of the steadfast love of the LORD.

-Isaiah 1:17 - Learn to do good; seek justice, correct oppression; bring justice to the fatherless, plead the widow's cause.

-Isaiah 30:18 - Therefore the LORD waits to be gracious to you, and therefore he exalts himself to show mercy to you. For the LORD is a God of justice; blessed are all those who wait for him.

-Isaiah 51:4-6 – "Give attention to me, my people, and give ear to me, my nation; for a law will go out from me, and I will set my justice for a light to the peoples. My righteousness draws near, my salvation has gone out, and my arms will judge the peoples; the coastlands hope for me, and for my arm they wait. Lift up your eyes to the heavens, and look at the earth beneath; for the heavens vanish like smoke, the earth will wear out like a garment, and they who dwell in it will die in like manner; but my salvation will be forever, and my righteousness will never be dismayed."

-Matthew 12:18 - Behold, my servant whom I have chosen, my beloved with whom my soul is well pleased. I will put my Spirit upon him, and he will proclaim justice to the Gentiles.

-Luke 18:7-8 - And will not God give justice to his elect, who cry to him day and night? Will he delay long over them? I tell you, he will give justice to them speedily. Nevertheless, when the Son of Man comes, will he find faith on earth?

-Romans 11:33-36 – Oh, the depth of the riches and wisdom and knowledge of God! How unsearchable are his judgments and how inscrutable his ways! "For who has known the mind of the Lord, or who has been his counselor? Or who has given a gift to him that he might be repaid?" For from him and through him and to him are all things. To him be glory forever. Amen.

Week 4 – Loving

As we approach this week, I realize that we have passed the one-third mark in this journey. I hope we have all started to see more clearly how the enemy has cast a negative light on the nature of God (including through the use of well-meaning religion). This has in turn robbed us of our receptivity and openness to God. Will you agree with me as we continue that any more of those formerly entrenched ideas will begin to be uprooted and replaced by better, larger, and more out-of-the-box ideas instead? No matter where we are in God currently, there is always further to go!

After some heavy topics the last few weeks, I am so excited about digging into this chapter on the love of God. It is such a substantial topic that it gets a whole week to itself, but it really could be the subject of an entire library! This is actually the specific area where God started working in me and reshaping my image of Him. Having been raised in church and Christian school, I had always heard that God loved me. In reality though, it had not really taken root in my heart. I believe this was because the concept of His love was coupled with a very real fear of Him and of my sin sending me to hell. So I went through the religious motions, all the while keeping my heart back from God, because I did not trust Him.

As a young adult who had become distanced from faith, I took a brief rebellious jaunt out into the world that left me absolutely broken. Having tasted a lot of the 'forbidden fruit' that did not end up being very fulfilling, I returned to God willing to give it another try. When I did, I began to be exposed to more and more teaching on grace and thus my resulting position of right standing in God's eyes, as well as the concept of the very real clash on earth between the Kingdoms of light and darkness. The whole story started to make a lot more sense, and I began to reconcile the attributes that describe God in the Bible with the ugliness of this world. Gradually, I began to open myself up to His love, which is when I was truly changed forever. I invite you on this same path this week. Allow your heart to be opened in unprecedented ways to comprehend God's deep love for you.

Heart Cries

How many times have you heard a love song on the radio or seen a romantic movie that left you saying, 'Yeah right, that does not happen in real life.' Perhaps

I am a bit of a cynic, but such over-the-top expressions of love have always seemed a bit of a stretch to me. Yet, they did come out of someone. Whether that person believed it possible or not, their heart cry for an unfathomable, non-judgmental, absolutely immersing kind of love cannot be denied. It has not been limited to one genre of entertainment or one era either. It continues to be made and remade in as many ways as people will consume.

Like other attributes of God, I believe we have been created with a portion of His love within us, and this is where these amazing expressions of love originate. So even if the fulfillment of this desire remains unrequited during our earthly lives, our hearts do not stop longing for it. Based on the plethora of such entertainment available, I have to conclude that there must be this greater love we were made for that is so satisfying, it may even leave our natural minds a bit nauseated at first. Have you ever considered that these depictions of love might just be possible, only between you and the God of the universe?

It may take some effort, but try the following exercise with me. Think of a favorite love song (preferably non-religious) and really focus in on the lyrics. Then begin to imagine that your Creator and

Redeemer actually feels that way about you. Holy Spirit has ministered such love and acceptance to me through various songs, experiences that have left me completely undone. My songs have run the gamut from Celine Dion to George Strait, but there has always been an amazing encounter within. Set this aside for a moment and find your song.

For this recovering skeptic and overachiever, I cannot tell you how big of a step it has been for me to begin receiving our God's perfect love in such deep and emotional ways. He has done and will continue to do it for me, and He will do the same for you. We just have to let Him. This is what we were made for, to love and be loved, with absolutely nothing held back.

Besides the entertainment angle described above, these deep heart cries for love can also be seen in the basic relational postures between men and women. The need is certainly expressed differently, but rarely do you see either gender's specific desire for love being met sufficiently to their liking. Women want to be pursued emotionally and relationally, while men want the physical bonding of sexual intimacy. Through both we can see that people are desperately seeking to fill a deep void of worth and love within themselves.

Human love, just like everything else natural on this earth, is a mere representation of the heavenly version. It is only a shadow of things to come. Even the most content and Godly of human relationships cannot begin to fully satisfy the reservoir that has been created in each of us for a supernatural kind of love.

Unfortunately, because people have had this supernatural reservoir empty for so long, they have begun to ignore their heart cry. I believe this is the pivotal point at which our passion and zeal begin to be snuffed out, and we attempt to operate independently of our hearts. Some of us have numbed ourselves, and some have engaged with other passions. Regardless of the coping mechanism, we are never going to come back to a place of wholeness until we bravely reopen this reservoir and ask for God Himself to fill it.

Beloved

Another interesting topic in this discussion is how the attribute of God's love is characterized or directed toward people throughout the Bible. Scripture repeatedly uses the term 'beloved' when referring to and addressing believers throughout both the Old and New Testaments.

[See Ephesians 5:1-2 - Therefore be imitators of God, as beloved children. And walk in love, as Christ loved us and gave himself up for us, a fragrant offering and sacrifice to God.]

The prefix 'be-' means thoroughly or to provide with. Notice how passive this prefix is. We as the beloved are to be thoroughly loved or provided with love according to this terminology. For contrast, note that the Bible does not address us as 'you who love God.' So many times we are trying to muster up a love for Him, when we are really only equipped to be on the receiving end. There are many worship songs and creeds that profess our human love for God with the best words we can find, but they still sound a bit hollow. We, as the created ones, are trying to communicate a heartfelt emotion to the Creator who actually defines it. Sounds a bit absurd when you say it like that, doesn't it? Only when we have experienced His immeasurable love poured into us, can we return it back to Him and then on to others.

[See I John 4:19 - We love because he first loved us.]

In fact, I believe this is one reason why we are all worn out. We keep incredibly busy trying to give away what we simply do not have. If you think about it, we as humans are consumable resources, while God is obviously not. Here is a great illustration of basic supply and demand: it only makes sense that we need to be provided with love from His inexhaustible supply, in order to love Him in return and meet the unending demands of humanity around us.

It is at this point that religious mindsets may begin to think this focus on receiving love is sounding a bit selfish. However, it really is not; it's just economics. If the supply and demand curves are out of balance, there is only one thing coming – collapse. Let's not allow old ideas to hold us back any longer in this way and cause the system to break down. It is time to freely receive from Him as the be-loved. He has more than enough to spare.

No Fear

I would like to cover one last aspect of this attribute of the love of God. As a child, I was inclined to be fearful. My parents were never sure of where this came from exactly, but it literally started within minutes of my birth. Being in a God-honoring family, I was naturally taught various Scriptures to help me overcome this fear. I did not come across a very important verse on fear though until sometime later in life.

[See I John 4:18 - There is no fear in love, but perfect love casts out fear. For fear has to do with punishment, and whoever fears has not been perfected in love.]

As I studied this Scripture as an adult, I realized that I had actually lived out this verse. Unfortunately because of some religious environments that our family had been in, I had become terrified of punishment from God. This fear had prevented me from receiving or being perfected in His love. It was only when I started to comprehend that God's judgment of sin had been completely satisfied on the body of Christ that I understood He was no longer out to punish anyone (to inflict a penalty for an offense). Jesus already took all of that on the cross.

[See Isaiah 53:4-5 - Surely he has borne our griefs and carried our sorrows; yet we esteemed him stricken, smitten by God, and afflicted. But he was pierced for our transgressions; he was crushed for our iniquities; upon him was the chastisement that brought us peace, and with his wounds we are healed.]

As we are God's children, He does still discipline or correct us. However, this is only for the purpose of our training and betterment, not our pain. I believe this is why my heart started to finally open up to His love, because I had begun to release the fear of Him. It was then that my perfection in love began, and it continues to this day.

I am reminded of the 90's skater brand, No Fear. Does anybody else remember this one? The company produced hats and shirts, all practically screaming with patterns and words that we were not afraid of anything. It is quite amusing to think about what a bluff these actually were, as teenagers across the country paraded around in them, desperately trying to look brave and cover up how they were really feeling about life. No matter how we may try to courageously frame even the hardest of circumstances, the only genuine place of living without fear is when we begin to receive and be made whole in perfect love.

So anytime I do notice myself acting in fear or in a bluffed-up fashion to cover the reality of my underlying fear, Holy Spirit is usually quick to get my attention and ask me what hidden area still has not been perfected in His love. The life of maturing in God is such a process, and I still find myself surprised when some new area gets uncovered and healed. As we move into next week on the attributes of God's goodness and faithfulness, there will be more opportunities to find issues where are not trusting His heart and still holding something back due to misunderstandings of Him.

L-O-V-E

If you were to ask me which of the attributes of God was the most important, I would say without hesitation that it is His love. No other attribute approached in isolation produces such immense transformation in the human heart. This week is an amazing opportunity to spend deliberate time asking God to give you a divine deposit of His love.

I could sit and stare at Ephesians 3 in the Scriptures all day long. I appreciate so much the word picture that is given in this chapter of our 'roots' growing down into His love.

[See Ephesians 3:17-19 - Then Christ will make his home in your hearts as you trust in him. Your roots will grow down into God's love and keep you strong. And may you have the power to understand, as all God's people should, how wide, how long, how high, and how deep his love is. May you experience

the love of Christ, though it is too great to understand fully. Then you will be made complete with all the fullness of life and power that comes from God.]

The purpose of a root system of any plant is to give it stability and strength even if natural conditions begin to threaten its existence. I recall a time when I was pulling weeds one fall after a particularly dry Texas summer. These were just the little weeds that grow in Bermuda grass regularly. I had often removed such weeds, so you can imagine my surprise on this occasion when the roots were much harder to pull. What I previously could have removed by bending over and grabbing with one hand, was now requiring both feet firmly planted and both hands pulling as hard as possible! Once I finally got them out, I saw they were probably five times as thick and long as ones I had seen before. Here it was the same environment of our yard and the same species from the surface, but these weeds were substantially more grounded.

As you focus on God's love this week and ask Him to fill you, imagine your personal spiritual root system getting thicker and thicker as you soak up all of Him that is possible. Let's expect to enjoy ourselves in His presence and also see marked growth as we become strong and grounded in His love!

[See Colossians 2:6-7 - Therefore, as you received Christ Jesus the Lord, so walk in him, rooted and built up in him and established in the faith, just as you were taught, abounding in thanksgiving.]

Week 4 Reflections & Meditations

Reflect: Recall a relationship in your life that you knew to be unhealthy. What were some of the marker moments or red flags that this was the case? Now describe what the opposite kind of love would have looked like.

Meditate: Glance through the Week 4 Scriptures and pick several to meditate on this week. Write them in the space below, make a notecard, or create a memo on your phone to keep them handy. Writing them helps, speaking them helps, and praying them to God helps most of all.

Apply: Get into your own highly personal routine of receiving God's love daily. Ask yourself about the particulars surrounding how you effectively receive love right now from those closest to you. How might this be translated into your relationship with God? Journal the details below.

Week 4 Scripture Listing

Heart Cry

-Psalm 31:16 - Make your face shine on your servant; save me in your steadfast love!

-Psalm 63:2-4 - So I have looked upon you in the sanctuary, beholding your power and glory. Because your steadfast love is better than life, my lips will praise you. So I will bless you as long as I live; in your name I will lift up my hands.

-Song of Solomon 4:7 - You are altogether beautiful, my love; there is no flaw in you.

-Song of Solomon 6:4-5 - You are beautiful as Tirzah, my love, lovely as Jerusalem, awesome as an army with banners. Turn away your eyes from me, for they overwhelm me—

-Zephaniah 3:17 - The LORD your God is in your midst, a mighty one who will save; he will rejoice over you with gladness; he will quiet you by his love; he will exult over you with loud singing.

-Romans 8:37-39 - No, in all these things we are more than conquerors through him who loved us. For I am sure that neither death nor life, nor angels nor rulers, nor things present nor things to come, nor powers, nor height nor depth, nor anything else in all creation, will be able to separate us from the love of God in Christ Jesus our Lord.

Beloved

-Song of Solomon 2:10-12 - My beloved speaks and says to me: "Arise, my love, my beautiful one, and come away, for behold, the winter is past; the rain is over and gone. The flowers appear on the earth, the time of singing has come, and the voice of the turtledove is heard in our land.

-Song of Solomon 7:10 - I am my beloved's, and his desire is for me.

-Jeremiah 31:3b - I have loved you with an everlasting love; therefore I have continued my faithfulness to you.

-John 15:9 - As the Father has loved me, so have I loved you. Abide in my love.

-1 John 3:1-3 - See what kind of love the Father has given to us, that we should be called children of God; and so we are.

-1 John 4:7-8 - Beloved, let us love one another, for love is from God, and whoever loves has been born of God and knows God. Anyone who does not love does not know God, because God is love.

-1 John 4:10-11 - In this is love, not that we have loved God but that he loved us and sent his Son to be the propitiation for our sins. Beloved, if God so loved us, we also ought to love one another.

No Fear

-Psalm 34:4 - I sought the LORD, and he answered me and delivered me from all my fears.

-Hosea 14:4 - I will heal their apostasy; I will love them freely, for my anger has turned from them.

-John 3:16-17 - For God so loved the world, that he gave his only Son, that whoever believes in him should not perish but have eternal life. For God did not send his Son into the world to condemn the world, but in order that the world might be saved through him.

-Romans 5:7-8 - For one will scarcely die for a righteous person—though perhaps for a good person one would dare even to die— but God shows his love for us in that while we were still sinners, Christ died for us.

-Hebrews 10:15-18 - And the Holy Spirit also bears witness to us; for after saying, "This is the covenant that I will make with them after those days, declares the Lord: I will put my laws on their hearts, and write them on their minds," then he adds, "I will remember their sins and their lawless deeds no more." Where there is forgiveness of these, there is no longer any offering for sin.

-I John 4:18 - There is no fear in love, but perfect love casts out fear. For fear has to do with punishment, and whoever fears has not been perfected in love.

Week 5 – Good & Faithful

Has it been surprising to see the word, meditation, included in every week's application questions? This word has often been hijacked by many new-age religions but is actually quite Biblical. Granted, sometimes this practice is encouraged in a direction other than towards the God of the Bible. But as long as our focus is correct, we will be missing out if we do not incorporate meditation into our spiritual relationship with God. Here are just a few verses on the topic.

[Joshua 1:8 - This Book of the Law shall not depart from your mouth, but you shall meditate on it day and night, so that you may be careful to do according to all that is written in it. For then you will make your way prosperous, and then you will have good success.]

[Psalm 77:12 - I will ponder all your work, and meditate on your mighty deeds.]

[Psalm 119:15 - I will meditate on your precepts and fix my eyes on your ways.]

The technical definition of meditation is time spent in quiet thought, reflection, or contemplation. So we need to be spending substantial amounts of time deliberately focusing on God, whether it is His works and ways, His promises, or His character. The world's tangible circumstances can practically scream at us so loudly, that it becomes very easy to switch over and move in the opposite direction of worry (defined as to torment oneself with or suffer from disturbing thoughts, fret, move with effort). How often do we mindlessly engage in the practice of worry as we are doing everyday things like dressing or driving?

When we notice this drift beginning, we must immediately stop ourselves and choose instead to meditate on God. When we make this decision, our minds are naturally quieted and we begin to elevate Him above our circumstances.

[See Isaiah 30:15 – For thus said the Lord GOD, the Holy One of Israel, "In returning and rest you shall be saved; in quietness and in trust shall be your strength."]

As we move forward into studying the goodness and faithfulness of God this week, I am asking Holy Spirit to help us keep our Biblical meditations front and center throughout our days and see what else God does in us!

Good

Good is a very commonly used word in the English language. Because of this, we can begin to glance right over it as one of the primary attributes of God and dismiss some of the powerful truths packed into it. The textbook definition of good is something or someone that is excellent, profitable, morally right, useful, or beneficial. While I certainly want to view God like that, I also like the way that the word is used often now in everyday conversations. Whether referring to a movie, a conversation, or a meal, 'that was good' has come to mean that some appetite has been satisfied (to fulfill the desires, expectations, needs, or demands of; give full contentment to).

This very physical way of thinking about goodness involves all of our five senses of seeing, hearing, smelling, tasting, and feeling. Receiving information through our physical senses rounds out the experience of a situation, taking it far beyond just the intellectual realm, and solidifying the memory as tangible and satisfying. In the same way, our appetites can also be fulfilled by our good God as we begin to fully experience Him. We can see this in the following verse.

[See Psalm 34:8 - Oh, taste and see that the LORD is good! Blessed is the man who takes refuge in him!]

I recently learned about an invention in progress that is attempting to create a vest that can receive information through the skin that would ordinarily be received by other senses. This would allow visual or auditory data to become available to blind and deaf people when wearing this vest by converting those colors/tones/etc. into sensations that can be understood by the skin. Seems a bit sci-fi, yes, but also very insightful. If this invention proves successful, previously undiscovered knowledge will become available to those who have been hindered by such physical limitations. They have always had to compensate through the use of their other senses.

Can we dare to expand our spiritual expectation of God in a similar way? What new knowledge and revelations might become available when we open up all of ourselves to Him? The Bible actually encourages us to do so in the passage above, 'Oh taste and see.' That goes much further than asking us to merely believe something with our minds. It is actually inviting us to experience His goodness in new and enjoyable ways. When we do so, we will also be less likely to fall into various temptations, because we will be so satisfied in Him that everything else that once attracted our appetites will begin to lose flavor.

This attribute of the goodness of God is also interesting, in that, it seems to encompass many of the other attributes. At the foundation of His justice, mercy, etc., is the fact that He is good. His provision of so many other things flows out of His goodness towards humanity. It is simply who He is. A great Biblical section displaying this truth is found in Exodus 33. Moses, one of the heroes of the Old Testament, was apprehensive about the task ahead of leading the nation of Israel out of Egypt. As he spoke with God about this and sought more confidence, he boldly asked to see God's glory. See God's response below.

[See Exodus 33:18-23 - Moses said, "Please show me your glory." And he said, "I will make all my GOODNESS pass before you and will proclaim before you my name 'The LORD.' And I will be gracious to whom I will be gracious, and will show mercy on whom I will show mercy. But," he said, "you cannot see my face, for man shall not see me and live." And the LORD said, "Behold, there is a place by me where you shall stand on the rock, and while my glory

passes by I will put you in a cleft of the rock, and I will
cover you with my hand until I have passed by. Then I
will take away my hand, and you shall see my back, but
my face shall not be seen."]

It is fascinating to see that God Himself equated
His glory with His goodness in this passage. A person's
glory is what they are honored and praised for or what
they are famous for. We can see that the goodness of
God is not just some window-dressing added to make
Him more appealing to us. It is actually His very
essence that passed by Moses that day and what He
wants to be known for on the earth! This specific
attribute is so important, because God knows that
unbelievers will be drawn to Him en masse when His
goodness and kindness are more fully revealed.

[See Romans 2:4 - Or do you presume on the
riches of his kindness and forbearance and patience,
not knowing that God's kindness is meant to lead you
to repentance?]

Unfortunately so many times people are
persuaded, guilted, or even lectured into God's family,
rather than by being led patiently by way of goodness
into His heart. That is the only path where we can
truly repent and be motivated to change in and of
ourselves. This is because He begins to be revealed to

us in new ways that are so remarkable and personal rather than condemning and distant.

I know my own lack of experience with the goodness of God is part of the reason my personal relationship with Him required such a transformation from dutiful to passionate. If we question His goodness deep down in our hearts as I did, we are not going to desire to be very close to Him. But as we clear up our misunderstandings and begin to be motivated by love rather than by fear, the depth of relationship that is possible increases exponentially (maybe even infinitely) because we finally trust His character and heart.

Faithful

Faithfulness is another attribute that strongly correlates to God's goodness, which is why it is included this week. We would never say that an intrinsically good person was someone who was flaky and always letting us down. Because of His goodness, we know that God must be counted as one who is faithful or true to His word. His faithfulness can also be described as steady, loyal, constant, reliable, trusted, believed.

It's also interesting to note that faithfulness is linked to God's love in many Scriptures. King David, the greatest worshipper the world has ever known and who God referred to as a man after His own heart, consistently associated the faithfulness of God with His steadfast love in the book of Psalms.

[See Psalm 117:1-2 - Praise the LORD, all nations! Extol him, all peoples! For great is his steadfast love toward us, and the faithfulness of the LORD endures forever. Praise the LORD!]

I believe this is because it is God's deep love that is always at the forefront of our encounters, waiting to be faithful to us. It is not that His holiness or jealousy will ever change either, but He knew we would need to be constantly reminded of His appealing and enduring love in the ongoing onslaught of the enemy's lies.

When you think about faithfulness, there is also the opposite attribute, which is faithlessness. It actually says specifically in the Bible that even when we have lost our faith, that God is still full of faith because He cannot deny Himself (His very nature).

[See 2 Timothy 2:11-13 – The saying is trustworthy, for: If we have died with him, we will also live with him; if we endure, we will also reign with him;

if we deny him, he also will deny us; if we are faithless,
he remains faithful—for he cannot deny himself.]

This has to be the strongest communication of
faithfulness – when one side of the relationship is
bearing so much more of the burden than the other
and will continue to do so regardless of the other's
choices. This very drama is actually played out in the
Bible in the book of Hosea. Hosea was a prophet of
God to Israel in the Old Testament. Early on in the
first chapter, God instructs Hosea to marry a prostitute
named Gomer, that this might be an illustration of
God's relationship with Israel.

Defying the customs and proper appearances of
the time, Hosea follows the instructions and marries
her. I'm sure this situation would get just as many
bewildered glances if it happened today! After having
children together, Gomer leaves Hosea and is
unfaithful with other men. Just as God pursues Israel
after her relationships with other gods, so Hosea also
pursues Gomer and brings her back into relationship.

This book of the Bible tunes into the very heart of
the Father and the unfathomable depths of His love,
despite the unfaithfulness of His chosen people. Of
course, let's not just point the finger at Israel though.
The Gomer in this story can describe each and every

one of us at times when we put Him on the shelf and pursue other passions. Yet, despite all of our shortcomings and faithlessness, God is still faithful and yearns for an intimate relationship with each of us. Because of the unconditional nature of this attribute, we can be ever so confident in His faithful heart. That no matter where we have been, as we turn to deliberately seek Him, He will be ready and waiting.

[See Hosea 6:3 - Oh, that we might know the Lord! Let us press on to know him. He will respond to us as surely as the arrival of dawn or the coming of rains in early spring.]

For every person out there, God encourages each of us to form an attitude of desiring Him and pressing onward, so that He can surely (firmly, unerringly) respond. If we do falter a bit or are even unfaithful to Him, we know that regardless He will still come after us! Let the principles of this story and the revealed heart of the faithfulness of God sink down deep into your spirit today. It is not ever because of anything you have done or will do. It is because of His very nature which will not be denied.

Is He Really?

The revelation of these two attributes is like a one-two punch at the enemy's distorted image of a mean spirited and distant God. What we actually have is a God who is so good and faithful, that it can even be to His detriment. Unlike us as short-sighted humans, He will only be who He is, regardless of our behavior. Our adversary knows this, so the best he can do is twist how we think of and relate to God. While God will always continue to be His good and faithful self, we tend to turn our backs on Him because we believe otherwise. Thus, we see the enemy's only strategy that will result in victory – our poor choices because of inaccurate information.

[See Hosea 4:6a – My people are destroyed for lack of knowledge.]

So I venture to ask, what circumstances have put a twinge in our hearts in this direction? No doubt there are many cruelties in the world vying for your mind's attention right now that He had no part in whatsoever (see Chapter 3). But could it possibly be less than that, maybe the delay of a long awaited dream or promise? This can be a very painful part of life, struggling to believe on the hard days when nothing seems to be moving. Often in religious circles, these are described as 'wilderness' seasons. While I do understand that term of feeling as if you are in the desert, there is a framework that I like a bit better.

It's what we can refer to as a time of the hum. What I mean by that is an under the surface knowing (or humming) that we are living below our potential. It is similar to discontent, but it's also a painful awareness that we are made for more. We feel this hum in our soul and spirit, but there is an actual biological phenomenon with this hum in eagles. When eagles are flying at low altitudes, they have a physical hum in their brain that reminds them to climb higher. Just like that, we were made to soar at incredible altitudes in our respective destinies with God. However, just like eagles, we cannot stay up there forever. We have to come down to eat, to catch another air current, etc.

So while this hum can certainly be agitating while at low altitudes, in reality it is our lifeline of hope, provided by a good and faithful God who has perfectly equipped us to live this life. That is precisely why I prefer this terminology to that of the wilderness; it has an implied relief to it. It also speaks to the glory we were all created for.

[See Psalm 8:5 - Yet you have made him (mankind) a little lower than the heavenly beings and crowned him with glory and honor.]

God's original intent was not for us to eek out an existence in a barren wasteland, but rather to be representations of His glory as we live as soaring overcomers in this life. Yet, these experiences in life do inevitably roll around for everyone, and we are left with a decision to make. Will we continue to believe in His goodness and faithfulness while we wait for the hum to subside, or will we begin to entertain the enemy's lies and question if God is really who He says He is?

The hum may be a health crisis, the delay of a dream to start a business, waiting for God to bring along that spouse you desire, watching a child struggle, or caring for an elderly relative. The list could go on and on, for as many who are reading this and the struggles they walk through. For me personally, it has been over the last nine years, during which time God has asked me to lay down any career aspirations and future plans to simply follow Him, wherever that might lead (to include the late-night writing sessions of this book). That may not sound painful to you but for a driven, doer such as myself, it can be tantamount to torture!

Whatever your particulars are, I will bet you are wishing them away and maybe even beginning to question God. He can have so much to say during these times, if we will come before Him and listen, rather than harden our hearts. I have found that even in these painful days of the hum, He is always there ready to pick up the pieces, listen to me, and reassure me of the path I am on that will soon lead to greater altitudes. If He is not going to give us our way 100% of the time (like any good parent knows not to do), then I would argue that this is certainly what goodness and faithfulness looks like while we wait.

Week 5 Reflections & Meditations

Reflect: Reminisce about a specific point in your past when you felt very satisfied across a broad range of desires. Maybe it was after a holiday meal with family, after a celebration concluding an accomplishment, etc. What was it about the circumstances that led to your fullness and contentment?

Meditate: Glance through the Week 5 Scriptures and pick several to meditate on this week. Write them in the space below, make a notecard, or create a memo on your phone to keep them handy. Writing them helps, speaking them helps, and praying them to God helps most of all.

Apply: While interacting with people this week, look out for opportunities to respond in an attitude of faithfulness, even if they are acting faithlessly toward you. If you have kids, I'd start right there! What does this relational stance require of you and your heart? Journal the details below.

Week 5 Scripture Listing

Good

-Psalm 31:19 - Oh, how abundant is your goodness, which you have stored up for those who fear you and worked for those who take refuge in you, in the sight of the children of mankind!

-Psalm 65:4 – Blessed is the one you choose and bring near, to dwell in your courts! We shall be satisfied with the goodness of your house, the holiness of your temple!

-Psalm 119:68 - You are good and do good; teach me your statutes.

-Psalm 145:9 - The LORD is good to all, and his mercy is over all that he has made.

-Jeremiah 31:13-14 - Then shall the young women rejoice in the dance, and the young men and the old shall be merry. I will turn their mourning into joy; I will comfort them, and give them gladness for sorrow. I will feast the soul of the priests with abundance, and my people shall be satisfied with my goodness, declares the LORD."

-Lamentations 3:25-26 - The LORD is good to those who wait for him, to the soul who seeks him. It is good that one should wait quietly for the salvation of the LORD.

-Nahum 1:7 - The LORD is good, a stronghold in the day of trouble; he knows those who take refuge in him.

-Zechariah 9:16-17a - On that day the LORD their God will save them, as the flock of his people; for like the jewels of a crown they shall shine on his land. For how great is his goodness, and how great his beauty!

-Acts 14:16-17 - In past generations he allowed all the nations to walk in their own ways. Yet he did not leave himself without witness, for he did good by giving you rains from heaven and fruitful seasons, satisfying your hearts with food and gladness.

-Romans 2:4 - Or do you presume on the riches of his kindness and forbearance and patience, not knowing that God's kindness is meant to lead you to repentance?

Faithful

-Psalm 33:4-5 - For the word of the LORD is upright, and all his work is done in faithfulness. He loves righteousness and justice; the earth is full of the steadfast love of the LORD.

-Psalm 36:5-6 – Your steadfast love, O LORD, extends to the heavens, your faithfulness to the clouds. Your righteousness is like the mountains of God; your judgments are like the great deep; man and beast you save, O LORD.

-Psalm 117:1-2 - Praise the LORD, all nations! Extol him, all peoples! For great is his steadfast love toward us, and the faithfulness of the LORD endures forever. Praise the LORD!

-Lamentations 3:22-24 - The steadfast love of the LORD never ceases; his mercies never come to an end; they are new every morning; great is your faithfulness. "The LORD is my portion," says my soul, "therefore I will hope in him."

-1 Corinthians 10:13 – No temptation has overtaken you that is not common to man. God is faithful, and he will not let you be tempted beyond your ability, but with the temptation he will also provide the way of escape, that you may be able to endure it.

-2 Thessalonians 3:3 - But the Lord is faithful. He will establish you and guard you against the evil one.

-2 Timothy 2:11-13 - The saying is trustworthy, for: If we have died with him, we will also live with him; if we endure, we will also reign with him; if we deny him, he also will deny us; if we are faithless, he remains faithful—for he cannot deny himself.

-Hebrews 10:23 - Let us hold fast the confession of our hope without wavering, for he who promised is faithful.

Week 6 – Holy & Beautiful

If there is one thing that I have become aware of as I work through this together with you, it would be the vast amount of God consciousness that is possible for every person. Getting my mind off myself and off my little universe turns out to be a very healthy thing! I wish there was room here to blow our minds with additional aspects of God through the use of other disciplines and studies, which would keep us all standing in complete awe of Him. For example, I once saw a devotional book that contained detailed pictures of new discoveries in outer space, accompanied by verses of Scripture. I was completely captivated by this approach to spending time with God. I would encourage you to keep an eye out for such books, documentaries, etc. Look especially for those that relate to your specific interests and meaningfully continue to reveal God's heart to your heart. There is no shortage to the areas of our lives where He can be found. We just have to be looking.

Holy and beautiful - it may not seem completely natural that these two attributes fit together, but it is a relationship I have begun to see as I have spent more time with Him. They are both attributes that, as they grow, have the ability to capture our very imaginations. Holy is defined as exalted or worthy of complete devotion, as one perfect in goodness and righteousness, regarded as deserving special respect or reverence. While beautiful is defined as possessing qualities that give great pleasure or satisfaction, delighting the senses or mind, excellence of its kind.

Holy

Holy. I tend to look to my historical impressions on this attribute of God for insight. Growing up with a strong emphasis on living in a Godly way, I always had the impression that being holy was this unobtainable thing, to the point of a strong negative connotation being created in my mind. If someone began to go down the road of discussing this characteristic, it was almost a guarantee that I was going to tune out. This was because it made me feel condemned and under pressure. Being the calculating temperament I am, it seemed to be an absolute waste of time to focus on something that I was never going to achieve anyway. It also did not make me think that I could be very close to God, because He was so holy and perfect which made Him practically unapproachable for me.

Many years after these ideas were formed and I began my trek back to God, I was worshipping in a church service when Holy Spirit showed me something amazing. He gave me a brief picture of the most dazzling and blinding light I had ever seen. It emanated out from a central point in all directions, while not lessening in its piercing intensity as it traveled. Not even a speck of darkness could be seen. It was pure, clean, sparkling light. I naturally inquired about what I was seeing and why it was important. I was impressed that this was God Himself or His very nature. As I pondered this, Holy Spirit began to bring up many of the Scriptures that discussed light.

[See 1 John 1:5 – This is the message we have heard from him and proclaim to you, that God is light, and in him is no darkness at all.]

As He shared this part of Himself with me that night, I began to understand that this light was the base existence of His holiness. He is someone who is so exalted, perfect, and worthy; there is simply nothing else that can be seen when in His presence but purity. This is also why He cannot tolerate the darkness of sin, no matter how small. It is not because He is mean or a prude, rather it is because darkness literally cannot coexist in His realm! Even the tiniest imperfection or shadow cannot remain in the path of such light; it immediately becomes consumed.

[See James 1:17 - Every good gift and every perfect gift is from above, coming down from the Father of lights with whom there is no variation or shadow due to change.]

[Also Hebrews 12:28-29 - Therefore let us be grateful for receiving a kingdom that cannot be shaken, and thus let us offer to God acceptable worship, with reverence and awe, for our God is a consuming fire.]

While I quickly recognized the consequences of approaching this brilliant light, it was so warm that it did not scare me away, unlike my previous understanding of holiness. Rather than being an attribute that isolated, it actually invited. It was in that moment that I understood why we all so desperately need Jesus. We were made to exist in that light with our Heavenly Father. It is our true home and all will recognize it the moment it is seen. But then the question remains – will we do what is necessary to safely approach God again? Because in our natural state, having been born into sin, none of us would make it an inch.

It is as simple as accepting the forgiveness provided for by the death and resurrection of Jesus and then submitting our lives to His authority. We will discuss these ideas more next week as we turn to ponder His mercy and grace. For now, suffice it to say, this decision eliminates all darkness in us and replaces it with the holiness of Jesus. Then we can be perfectly at home in God's presence, wearing our own light filled robes of righteousness.

[See Ephesians 5:25-27 – Husbands, love your wives, as Christ loved the church and gave himself up for her, that he might sanctify her, having cleansed her by the washing of water with the word, so that he might present the church to himself in splendor, without spot or wrinkle or any such thing, that she might be holy and without blemish.]

[Also Isaiah 61:10 – I will greatly rejoice in the LORD; my soul shall exult in my God, for he has clothed me with the garments of salvation; he has covered me with the robe of righteousness.]

Gazing upon this brilliance, I now desired to thank God for His holiness rather than despise Him for it. He wants everyone to be there with Him in this perfect light. Since He knew we could not do it on our own, He sent Jesus to pave the way back for us. We simply have to surrender our will. No other effort is needed. And just like that, our holiness is 'achieved' (says the over-achiever). We can live as pure and set apart for Him all the days of our lives until we reach heaven, stand in His light, and shout with thankfulness together: holy, holy, holy is the Lord God Almighty!

Beautiful

Turning now to examine the beautiful aspect of God, I begin to think of the passages of Scripture that describe His majesty, the wonders of creation, or the riches of heaven. This is a perfectly reasonable place for our minds to go because of our typical ideas of beauty. We could certainly afford to spend more time meditating on these parts of Him. However, when I look at the definition of beautiful (possessing qualities that give great pleasure or satisfaction, delighting the senses or mind, excellence of its kind), I cannot help but think that something is missing. I believe this is because there is an intrinsic aspect of beauty that is difficult to put into words.

I remember reading a few years ago about a study that was done in this very area, where researchers were trying to analyze the key qualities of the human face that would be considered beautiful to a sample of people. The results showed that approximately ninety percent of participants chose based on the characteristic of symmetry. Symmetry is a geometric term that means being made up of exactly similar parts facing each other or around an axis. To say it more simply, symmetry is having balanced proportions. I have long thought back to that study and how our human brains are constantly analyzing and assessing beauty based on this quality, but most people probably do not even realize it.

Then one day it hit me, as Holy Spirit nudged in this direction, that symmetry is a tremendous part of God's beauty as well. He is a very orderly being. You have to look no further than the cycles and seasons of creation to understand this. Whether it is the human life cycle or the movements of the planets or the ocean tides, we can see that He has patterns and ways of doing things that will always remain. The Bible itself, which is His Word, also has tremendous amounts of symmetry that are fascinating. While we may not be able to specify that this is part of why we find Him beautiful, it seems that our minds are attracted to this attribute if even at a subconscious level.

The study mentioned above theorized that this trend toward symmetry was for evolutionary purposes.

They concluded that perhaps survival of the fittest mode made the human brain find balanced proportions attractive. This led to an overall assessment of good health for purposes of selecting a suitable mate. In other words, evaluating symmetry (beauty) was a way of minimizing risk. I agree with them on this point! God's cyclical nature or symmetry is beautiful to us, because it reveals that He is a safe place that can be trusted. Just as we trust that the sun is going to come up every day or that spring will always arrive after winter.

[See Isaiah 50:1-2 - The Mighty One, God the LORD, speaks and summons the earth from the rising of the sun to its setting. Out of Zion, the perfection of beauty, God shines forth.]

Beauty also seems to be partly based upon the frequency with which we have observed something. We tend to find rare phenomena, whether it is an unusual sunset or a scarce breed of animal, to be more beautiful than commonplace ones. Here is another way we can draw a parallel to our magnificent God. He is the only one of His kind; it does not get any more rare than that. Perhaps this is another reason why He desires for us to seek Him out personally, because He knows that we will appreciate and treasure such encounters far more than we would something that just came to us every day.

While we can certainly comprehend beholding beauty in a natural sense, it can be difficult to imagine 'gazing' upon God in a spiritual sense. A good exercise for all of us would be to spend time setting our minds and hearts on Him in the same way you would set your eyes on a physical object of beauty. We should go over and over the details and intricacies we notice, trying to take them all in, and making an effort to commit them to memory. These revelations can often be so deeply personal, you'll want to preserve them to recall for another day!

Maximum Effectiveness

I am not sure about you, but I know that I'm able to think better and work more effectively in a clean (holy) and orderly (beautiful) environment as opposed to a dirty and disorderly one. It is as if my mind knows the difference between safe and threatening based upon these characteristics. Such an ideal environment can put any self protection instincts aside to strictly focus on the task at hand.

In a similar way, I believe we will be at our best when our spirits have become fully immersed in the holiness and beauty of God. The presence of these qualities can put us completely at ease, because we know there is nothing left for us to do! Everything is already in order, so now we can be single-minded in our assignments for Him.

Occasionally, I will take a step back and observe human behavior and the mechanics of relationships. While I know that we are all living from some level of brokenness even as we grow and heal, I have particularly noticed how tricky it is to be in relationship with people who live from a chronically wounded place. In these situations, the ground always seems to be shifting and something inevitably ends up hurting feelings in even the smallest of ways. As I prayed and sought wisdom about one of these very relationships, Holy Spirit showed me that this is what God deals with in His relationship with each and every one of us. Our naturally wounded state can make us very hard to communicate with, as we become either withdrawn or defensive in our interactions with Him.

I had to marvel and think about what a difficult job God has and how blessed we are to be on the receiving end of our relationship with Him. We never have to occupy our time or energy with 'handling' Him or making sure He is 'okay.' His holy and beautiful nature makes Him the epitome of a completely safe relationship partner, which frees all of us to live our lives with maximum usefulness and fulfillment.

This has to be one of my favorite revelations that has emerged from this writing – that He loves to set us up for success in this way. Watching His kids not only soar, but enjoy the journey with Him safely by our side, is one of His greatest passions. Set your focus on God's holiness and beauty this week, and let's all cultivate a greater understanding of our safety and freedom in Him.

Week 6 Reflections & Meditations

Reflect: Let's play a word association game! Read the following sentences and jot down the first person, place, or thing that comes to mind. When I say holy, you say _____? When I say beautiful, you say _____? Are these positive or negative associations in your mind?

Meditate: Glance through the Week 6 Scriptures and pick several to meditate on this week. Write them in the space below, make a notecard, or create a memo on your phone to keep them handy. Writing them helps, speaking them helps, and praying them to God helps most of all.

Apply: Watch for points in your week when you are tempted to isolate or withdraw, either from others or from God. Take a moment when you realize this to focus on what the lie could be that is making you feel unwelcome rather than invited in. Journal the details below.

Week 6 Scripture Listing

Holy

-2 Samuel 23:4 - He dawns on them like the morning light, like the sun shining forth on a cloudless morning, like rain that makes grass to sprout from the earth.

-Psalm 36:9 - For with you is the fountain of life; in your light do we see light.

-Psalm 99:1-3 - The LORD reigns; let the peoples tremble! He sits enthroned upon the cherubim; let the earth quake! The LORD is great in Zion; he is exalted over all the peoples. Let them praise your great and awesome name! Holy is he!

-Isaiah 6:1-3 – In the year that King Uzziah died I saw the Lord sitting upon a throne, high and lifted up; and the train of his robe filled the temple. Above him stood the seraphim. Each had six wings: with two he covered his face, and with two he covered his feet, and with two he flew. And one called to another and said: "Holy, holy, holy is the LORD of hosts; the whole earth is full of his glory!"

-John 8:12 - Again Jesus spoke to them, saying, "I am the light of the world. Whoever follows me will not walk in darkness, but will have the light of life."

-1 Thessalonians 5:5 - For you are all children of light, children of the day. We are not of the night or of the darkness.

-Hebrews 7:26-27 – For it was indeed fitting that we should have such a high priest, holy, innocent, unstained, separated from sinners, and exalted above the heavens. He has no need, like those high priests, to offer sacrifices daily, first for his own sins and then for those of the people, since he did this once for all when he offered up himself.

-Revelation 22:5 - And night will be no more. They will need no light of lamp or sun, for the Lord God will be their light, and they will reign forever and ever.

Beautiful

-Genesis 8:22 - While the earth remains, seedtime and harvest, cold and heat, summer and winter, day and night, shall not cease.

-Job 37:22 – Out of the north comes golden splendor; God is clothed with awesome majesty.

-Psalm 27:4 – One thing have I asked of the LORD, that will I seek after: that I may dwell in the house of the LORD all the days of my life, to gaze upon the beauty of the LORD and to inquire in his temple.

- Psalm 50:1-2 – The Mighty One, God the LORD, speaks and summons the earth from the rising of the sun to its setting. Out of Zion, the perfection of beauty, God shines forth.

-Psalm 96:5-6 – For all the gods of the peoples are worthless idols, but the LORD made the heavens. Splendor and majesty are before him; strength and beauty are in his sanctuary.

-Psalm 104:19 – He made the moon to mark the seasons; the sun knows its time for setting.

-Song of Solomon 5:10-16 - My beloved is radiant and ruddy, distinguished among ten thousand. His head is the finest gold; his locks are wavy, black as a raven. His eyes are like doves beside streams of water, bathed in milk, sitting beside a full pool. His cheeks are like beds of spices, mounds of sweet-smelling herbs. His lips are lilies, dripping liquid myrrh. His arms are rods of gold, set with jewels. His body is polished ivory, bedecked with sapphires. His legs are alabaster columns, set on bases of gold. His appearance is like Lebanon, choice as the cedars. His mouth is most sweet, and he is altogether desirable. This is my beloved and this is my friend, O daughters of Jerusalem.

Safety & Freedom

-Psalm 4:8 - In peace I will both lie down and sleep; for you alone, O LORD, make me dwell in safety.

-Psalm 84:11-12 - For the LORD God is a sun and shield; the LORD bestows favor and honor. No good thing does he withhold from those who walk uprightly. O LORD of hosts, blessed is the one who trusts in you!

-John 8:36 - So if the Son sets you free, you will be free indeed.

-2 Corinthians 3:17 - Now the Lord is the Spirit, and where the Spirit of the Lord is, there is freedom.

Week 7 – Merciful & Gracious

Here we are embarking on week number seven in this adventure. Often, books like these are categorized as spiritual or Christian growth. When we consider growth in our relationship with God, I believe we often couch it in the realm of personal responsibility. However when you really think about it, no living thing can actually make itself grow! A little child cannot squint their eyes, flex their muscles, and get bigger – and neither can any plant or animal. Atheists would say that organism growth just occurs naturally through cell division, but we know that God is the one making this complicated process happen. Regardless, we can all agree that it is not a function of the organism willing it to occur.

Perhaps a better term for our understanding these resources in our lives would be spiritual nurturing. To nurture is to care for and encourage growth or development. That is what God is doing in each and every one of us as we follow Him. Yes, we must do our part; but it is more in our cooperation than in our initiation. We were not made to carry the burden of the responsibility. The sooner we realize that He is the One performing the nurturing, the sooner we will be free from our self-imposed pressures and able to grow instead from a place of rest.

[See Matthew 11:28-30 – Come to me, all who labor and are heavy laden, and I will give you rest. Take my yoke upon you, and learn from me, for I am gentle and lowly in heart, and you will find rest for your souls. For my yoke is easy, and my burden is light.]

This truth is seen so clearly in God's attributes of mercy and grace. These characteristics blatantly highlight that He has taken on the full responsibility of providing what we need, so we are left only to receive His perfect provision.

Merciful

Mercy is defined as compassion or forgiveness shown toward someone, especially when it is within one's power to punish or harm; performed out of a desire to relieve suffering; and motivated by compassion. God's mercy is the attribute that ultimately sent Jesus to the earth on a mission to rescue us out of our sinful state. It was God's compassion and desire to relieve our suffering that caused Him to offer up Jesus as a substitute for us.

[See Ephesians 2:4-7 – But God, being rich in mercy, because of the great love with which he loved us, even when we were dead in our trespasses, made us alive together with Christ—by grace you have been saved—and raised us up with him and seated us with him in the heavenly places in Christ Jesus, so that in the coming ages he might show the immeasurable riches of his grace in kindness toward us in Christ Jesus.]

The original sin committed by Adam and Eve in the Garden of Eden put all of mankind under the curse of sin and death. All of the tragedy and pain that we now see trickle down from this curse. As a result, the world we live in can be an extremely ugly place. For those that would philosophically question and say, 'How can a loving God allow such suffering?' The answer is that He cannot. His heart aches along with ours at the brokenness in the world. That is why His mercy had to create a way of escape. So Jesus came into this world, stood in our place, and took the punishment for our sin. Now anyone who calls on His name will be saved and brought out from under the curse!

[See Galatians 3:13 - Christ redeemed us from the curse of the law by becoming a curse for us—for it is

written, "Cursed is everyone who is hanged on a tree"—]

The punishment that Jesus bore on the cross was so much more than just the physical pain of the crucifixion. He had to actually become sin, so that we could become righteousness. Imagine every dark thing that has ever occurred was placed on His earthly frame that day. Every murder, rape, theft, lie, or even something as simple as a mean thought, He carried it all. Is it any wonder that the Scriptures tell us that His body became so disfigured in that moment that it was unrecognizable?

[See Isaiah 52:13-15 - Behold, my servant shall act wisely; he shall be high and lifted up, and shall be exalted. As many were astonished at you—his appearance was so marred, beyond human semblance, and his form beyond that of the children of mankind— so shall he sprinkle many nations; kings shall shut their mouths because of him; for that which has not been told them they see, and that which they have not heard they understand.]

The opposite of mercy is ruthlessness or cruelty. It means taking pleasure in causing pain or suffering. This is exactly the nature of the enemy, as he operates in direct opposition to the character of God. When I picture the 'beyond human semblance' body of Jesus, I soberly realize that it was not only God's judgment for sin that was exhausted on His body that day. The cruelty that the enemy intended for us through sin was exhausted on Him as well. For me, this horrible image stirs up such a righteous passion within, to not leave any of God's merciful provision on the table. I do not want to insult or disrespect any part of the beautiful offering of Jesus by not utilizing everything that He bought and paid for when He stood in my place. This is true whether it involves salvation, peace, joy, healing, or blessing.

The following quote came to mind as I was writing this week: 'Experience is a cruel teacher.' Indeed it is, if we set off into the world determined to experience things for ourselves. When we choose to act rebelliously or even independently, we are opening ourselves up to attacks of the enemy, who has no problem teaching us through cruelty. But if we will come to God and simply receive His gift of mercy, we can be taught instead by His gentle wisdom. Jesus willingly allowed His body to be mangled for us in order to relieve our suffering. The enemy's cruelty does not need to be experienced by anyone else ever again!

Gracious

Often the attribute of graciousness is boiled down to the unmerited favor of God - His giving all of us what we do not deserve. While having this favor is certainly comforting and helpful in and of itself, I believe there is more that can be unpacked here. An additional definition of grace is simple elegance or refinement of movement. A few synonyms are elegance, poise, and finesse.

As I am currently starting a new fitness program, these terms make me contemplate the extreme amount of underlying muscle tone and strength that would be necessary to have such control! We know that God is all-powerful, so it is logical that He is capable of moving in such a way with great ease. Here is an excerpt from Job 38-39 that gives a beautiful description of the finesse with which God breathed creation.

[See Job 38:4-12 - Where were you when I laid the foundation of the earth? Tell me, if you have understanding. Who determined its measurements—surely you know! Or who stretched the line upon it? On what were its bases sunk, or who laid its cornerstone, when the morning stars sang together and

all the sons of God shouted for joy? Or who shut in the sea with doors when it burst out from the womb, when I made clouds its garment and thick darkness its swaddling band, and prescribed limits for it and set bars and doors, and said, 'Thus far shall you come, and no farther, and here shall your proud waves be stayed'? Have you commanded the morning since your days began, and caused the dawn to know its place?]

What an amazing train of thought - to picture God's strength and power on display with such elegance and grace. I believe this is what He wants for all of us to partake of as well. In the physical realm though, we cannot have this elegant, refined, poised, finessed movement without having tremendous strength throughout our bodies. This strength has to be built up over time; it's not just a one-time download. Could it be that we may have to develop the grace we receive from God in this same way?

[See 2 Peter 3:18 - But grow in the grace and knowledge of our Lord and Savior Jesus Christ. To him be the glory both now and to the day of eternity. Amen.]

[Also John 1:16 - For from his fullness we have all received, grace upon grace.]

These Scriptures appear to indicate so. It's as if there are superseding places to go other than where we are presently in our understanding of grace. I find it interesting to reexamine this passage in Matthew 11, except this time as stated in The Message version of the Bible.

[See Matthew 11:28-30 (MSG) - "Are you tired? Worn out? Burned out on religion? Come to me. Get away with me and you'll recover your life. I'll show you how to take a real rest. Walk with me and work with me—watch how I do it. Learn the unforced rhythms of grace. I won't lay anything heavy or ill-fitting on you. Keep company with me and you'll learn to live freely and lightly."]

This description of grace as unforced rhythms most definitely points to an ease of movement that He wants for us, which will only come through inner strength. As we work together with God in going through our life circumstances, we build more and more spiritual muscle that enables us to be more powerful believers. God wants us to become so adept in grace, as He is, that we will be able to function in all circumstances with a poise and ease that will make unbelievers stop and wonder. Reflecting this attribute of His in greater measure will make an incredible impact on a watching world!

Pity or Honor?

In summary, I like to think of mercy as the payment and grace as the empowerment. Both are completely undeserved and provided freely to us out of the overflow of our very merciful and gracious Father, but they each have a different emphasis. We cannot begin to walk in the power of His grace until we have first received His payment of mercy. Of all the attributes we have studied, I think these might be the least misunderstood in general. However, the motivation driving them seems to be where the wires get crossed.

It appears that many believers maintain that God grants us His mercy and grace out of some sort of pity. As a result of this erroneous foundational thinking, we can end up approaching God like beggars, hoping that He will provide us with something...anything. The Bible specifically tells us to have a different posture though. He actually wants us to approach Him with boldness, as beloved children, knowing that we will receive.

[See Hebrews 4:16 – Let us then with confidence draw near to the throne of grace, that we may receive mercy and find grace to help in time of need.]

Be aware that when we start to speak in these terms, there may be some shocked reactions. It's as if people are thinking, 'How dare they be so grandiose in their opinion of their standing with God?' If considering ourselves as confident and loved children is grandiose, the Scripture below is off the charts.

[See Psalm 8:3-6 - When I look at your heavens, the work of your fingers, the moon and the stars, which you have set in place, what is man that you are mindful of him, and the son of man that you care for him? Yet you have made him a little lower than the heavenly beings and crowned him with glory and honor. You have given him dominion over the works of your hands; you have put all things under his feet.]

Did you catch all of that? If not, please go back and read it again. The Bible describes us as being crowned with glory and honor, being given dominion over the works of God's hands, and having all things put under our feet. The small time attitude, normally camouflaged as humbleness, that dominates much of religious thinking is a lie from the enemy meant to keep us ineffective and unfruitful. Of course, we must

133

keep a watch against pride and remain submitted to Him. But if we are going to live the big and impactful lives that God has destined for us, we must break free of old mindsets and receive the truth of our priceless value in God's eyes.

A final thought on this point of pity versus honor - if the traditions and thinking of the past seem too difficult to overcome in this regard, there is one more piece of the puzzle that should clearly reveal God's original intentions for us. It has been said that the value of something is based upon what will be paid for it. God paid the high, incalculable price of the innocent blood of His Son, Jesus, to redeem mankind. It is as if He put a price tag on each one of us with a dollar sign followed by the infinity symbol! Let's all work on reforming our thinking this week, so that His mercy and grace flow to us from a place of value and honor and not one of pity.

[See Isaiah 43:4 - Because you are precious in my eyes, and honored, and I love you, I give men in return for you, peoples in exchange for your life.]

His Right, Our Left

As we come to the end of these attributes, our natural minds can entertain the idea that it cannot possibly be this easy. Perhaps we think we need to do more or be more to earn His mercy and grace. These thoughts are lies from the enemy aimed right at our vulnerable hearts and meant to prevent us from accepting these free gifts from God. Our striving natures cause us to want to do something. God knows this and does not leave us feeling unfulfilled. He very much wants to involve us.

An excellent illustration of our partnership with Him is seen in the many Scriptural references to the right hand of God. Most people are right-handed, so this is most often considered to be the dominant or strong hand. Once after I had received a prophecy about the right hand of God upholding me, Holy Spirit quietly asked me what hand of mine would then be necessary? It would obviously be my left, in order to join properly to His right hand. He deeply desires our input and our involvement. It just needs to come from this submitted 'left-hand' place that is ready to receive, in order to perfectly fit into His powerful right hand.

Week 7 Reflections & Meditations

Reflect: In your past, what have been some marked moments of receiving mercy or enduring cruelty? Could it be possible for these situations to ever flow from the same source? Pinpoint a distinct memory when you were not poised (full of grace). Has your subsequent spiritual growth changed how you would act in a similar circumstance?

Meditate: Glance through the Week 7 Scriptures and pick several to meditate on this week. Write them in the space below, make a notecard, or create a memo on your phone to keep them handy. Writing them helps, speaking them helps, and praying them to God helps most of all.

Apply: Evaluate your ability this week in receiving honor and free gifts, with nothing due in return. What have you noticed about your reluctance? What does freedom from this posture look like in your every day? Journal the details below.

Week 7 Scripture Listing

Merciful

-Psalm 23:6 – Surely goodness and mercy shall follow me all the days of my life, and I shall dwell in the house of the LORD forever.

- Isaiah 55:6-9 - Seek the LORD while he may be found; call upon him while he is near; let the wicked forsake his way, and the unrighteous man his thoughts; let him return to the LORD, that he may have compassion on him, and to our God, for he will abundantly pardon. For my thoughts are not your thoughts, neither are your ways my ways, declares the LORD. For as the heavens are higher than the earth, so are my ways higher than your ways and my thoughts than your thoughts.

-Ephesians 2:4-7 – But God, being rich in mercy, because of the great love with which he loved us, even when we were dead in our trespasses, made us alive together with Christ—by grace you have been saved—and raised us up with him and seated us with him in the heavenly places in Christ Jesus, so that in the coming ages he might show the immeasurable riches of his grace in kindness toward us in Christ Jesus.

-Hebrews 10:12-14 - But when Christ had offered for all time a single sacrifice for sins, he sat down at the right hand of God, waiting from that time until his enemies should be made a footstool for his feet. For by a single offering he has perfected for all time those who are being sanctified.

Gracious

-John 1:16-17 - For from his fullness we have all received, grace upon grace. For the law was given through Moses; grace and truth came through Jesus Christ.

-Acts 20:32 - And now I commend you to God and to the word of his grace, which is able to build you up and to give you the inheritance among all those who are sanctified.

-Romans 5:17 - For if, because of one man's trespass, death reigned through that one man, much more will those who receive the abundance of grace and the free gift of righteousness reign in life through the one man Jesus Christ.

-1 Corinthians 15:10 - But by the grace of God I am what I am, and his grace toward me was not in vain. On the contrary, I worked harder than any of them, though it was not I, but the grace of God that is with me.

-Ephesians 2:8-9 – For by grace you have been saved through faith. And this is not your own doing; it is the gift of God, not a result of works, so that no one may boast.

-2 Peter 3:18 - But grow in the grace and knowledge of our Lord and Savior Jesus Christ. To him be the glory both now and to the day of eternity. Amen.

Honor

-Genesis 1:27 - So God created man in his own image, in the image of God he created him; male and female he created them.

-Psalm 16:3 – As for the saints in the land, they are the excellent ones, in whom is all my delight.

-John 3:16-17 - For God so loved the world, that he gave his only Son, that whoever believes in him should not perish but have eternal life. For God did not send his Son into the world to condemn the world, but in order that the world might be saved through him.

-Romans 8:31-32 - What then shall we say to these things? If God is for us, who can be against us? He who did not spare his own Son but gave him up for us all, how will he not also with him graciously give us all things?

-1 Peter 1:18-19 - Knowing that you were ransomed from the futile ways inherited from your forefathers, not with perishable things such as silver or gold, but with the precious blood of Christ, like that of a lamb without blemish or spot.

His Right Hand

-Psalm 63:8 - My soul clings to you; your right hand upholds me.

-Psalm 98:1 - Oh sing to the LORD a new song, for he has done marvelous things! His right hand and his holy arm have worked salvation for him.

-Isaiah 41:10 - Fear not, for I am with you; be not dismayed, for I am your God; I will strengthen you, I will help you, I will uphold you with my righteous right hand.

-Hebrews 1:3 - He (Jesus) is the radiance of the glory of God and the exact imprint of his nature, and he upholds the universe by the word of his power. After making purification for sins, he sat down at the right hand of the Majesty on high.

Week 8 – Peaceful & Joyful

Even while we focus on these breathtaking, heavenly matters, I know they can be in rather stark contrast to the mundane and often difficult world in which we reside. However, these thoughts are not meant to be kept in a separate reality that runs parallel with our lives. If they stay in that detached place, we are truly wasting our time. Instead we must bring these truths into practical use, as they can actually be the difference makers in how well we function when we come up against adversity.

This week as I was rolling these ideas around in my mind, I looked out the window into the backyard and saw our four and five year-old sons on the trampoline. Ordinarily, they are always a fun sight to see as they bounce, laugh, and roll in every direction. But on this day, they were wearing their handmade, red, satin capes that were a present from their grandma. Watching their utter joy as they enacted every superhero dream with their capes flapping in the wind behind them, I couldn't stop smiling with happiness. I know that our Father God wants us all to live and dream just as exuberantly as the boys were that day.

Life can have such a tendency to cause us to hang up our capes and live ordinary, 'realistic' lives, and understandably so. There are days when I hear from multiple people about extremely difficult family, health, or job situations. When these times happen, we must come back to our own unique moments in His presence. This is what practical use looks like: allowing the marked contrast of what we have come to believe versus what we see to motivate us to put our capes back on and fight another day. The following Scripture gives us a great example of how to encourage ourselves by remembering our past experiences with God.

[See Psalm 42:5-6 – Why are you cast down, O my soul, and why are you in turmoil within me? Hope in God; for I shall again praise him, my salvation and my God. My soul is cast down within me; therefore I remember you from the land of Jordan and of Hermon, from Mount Mizar.]

Two attributes of God that can be powerful as we cheer ourselves onward are His peace and joy. Peace is defined as freedom from disturbance, quiet, and tranquility. Joy is known as a feeling of great pleasure and happiness. The combination of these two reveal a

God who truly enjoys Himself and corrects any false idea of Him being boring or stoic.

<u>Peaceful</u>

A few synonyms for peace are calm, quiet, serenity, order, and stability. Isn't it interesting that we have already studied order and stability as we examined God from other angles? I continue to be amazed at how this shows the consistency with which He reveals His character, even through differing facets.

One synonym we have not examined yet is calm, which can mean without irritation or inflammation. That is a very visual word – inflamed. I start to picture physical redness, puffiness, or tenderness. I also begin to think of what might be called 'inflammatory' situations in which we find ourselves struggling to remain calm. Knowing that God is the definition of peace means that He is calm regardless of what is happening. He cannot be driven out of this place. We have all met individuals who enjoy pushing other people's buttons. God's buttons cannot be pushed, even by the most gifted of irritators. He simply remains. Now that is something to ponder and stand in awe of!

[See 2 Thessalonians 3:16 - Now may the Lord of peace himself give you peace at all times in every way. The Lord be with you all.]

So where do your thoughts go when you consider this attribute? Do images of tranquil beach scenes or quiet mountain views come to mind? These are places that encourage us to rest and relax and slow down from what can be the frenzied pace of life. We pine for such locales because of this part of God that we desire. Although I know if I spend any extended amount of time in these settings, I do get a bit bored. I think that is the specific delineation of peace that is important: God is not sitting around doing nothing. He is occupied with meaningful activity while still maintaining a restful attitude. Solomon, who was King David's son and is considered to be the wisest and richest man who ever lived, learned this truth and spoke of it in the verses below.

[See Ecclesiastes 2:22-24a - What has a man from all the toil and striving of heart with which he toils beneath the sun? For all his days are full of sorrow, and his work is a vexation. Even in the night his heart does not rest. This also is vanity. There is nothing better for a person than that he should eat and drink and find enjoyment in his toil.]

We can also see this balance clearly in the ministry of Jesus by even a brief overview of the gospel accounts. He was always on the move, helping people along the way, yet never in a frantic or turbulent state. This intersection would be an amazing place for us all to live: engaged in fulfilling work while having the internal tranquility of rest.

We understand from our examination of peace so far that God remains consistently calm and that He is always pushing forward, yet in a relaxed way. As I consider this, I realize that the Bible makes several references comparing peace to a river, which is a body of water that has these same characteristics.

[See Isaiah 48:18 - Oh that you had paid attention to my commandments! Then your peace would have been like a river, and your righteousness like the waves of the sea.]

Since the Bible makes this direct link, let's examine some other natural details about rivers: they carry water from the source downward, their smooth surface can belie strong under-currents, they wear down objects in their pathway over time (even incredibly hard things like rock), they seem to naturally find the correct path as they travel and make adjustments, the course they follow creates a riverbed which can then accommodate more water as it deepens. The comparisons with our spiritual walk that can be drawn here are so vast, I almost don't know where to begin.

Perhaps the best place would be to imagine what it would be like to have God's river of peace coursing through us. We transport life giving hydration from God the source to others. We can look peaceful and still, while at the same time, having powerful force churning underneath the surface. We can wear through impossible obstacles with consistency and forward motion over time. We can find God's best path for our lives as we follow Him and make adjustments. We can become even greater influencers as we grow in depth and width. The fulfillment of all of these will come through the avenue of developing in the peace of God. I am afraid that we may have misunderstood this attribute of His to be a passive, weak thing – when in reality it may be one of the most powerful forces we have.

<u>Joyful</u>

This characteristic holds special meaning for me, since it is at the root of part of my given name. Of course, wouldn't you know it, it is a revelation of God that the enemy has always opposed. Quick side note – do take the time to learn the meanings and nuances of your full name. Whether or not parents realize it, God has a hand in naming every person. I can almost guarantee that it holds clues to your future and destiny, which the enemy would prefer to keep you in the dark about. Growing in the attribute of joy is very powerful for me, because it is what God has spoken over me since I was born. I know that there is a similar touch point contained in the name of every person reading this book as well.

Now, back to joy. The term itself may be a bit hollow in our modern English. It sounds like a religious word, so we tend to leave it in that context. Although as we saw in the introduction, it is actually defined as great pleasure and happiness. This is hardly terminology you would hear in most churches. Yet, the Bible actually links joy with pleasure in one of my favorite verses.

[See Psalm 16:11 - You make known to me the path of life; in your presence there is fullness of joy; at your right hand are pleasures forevermore.]

Seriously, what is not to love about this verse! Life. Joy. Pleasures. Forever. It can be difficult for us to think of the God of the universe in this way, partly because of the lies of the enemy and partly because we have put Him in our little boxes that we can understand. Similar to the chapter on love though, we know that He is deeply joyful because we can see it in the heart cry of all of us.

Humanity as a whole is desperate to have some fun, enjoy a good laugh, and experience real happiness. Just look at our sitcoms, movies, night-clubs, restaurants, vacation spots, etc. All of these past times are actually the hollow ones though, as they may provide a fleeting moment, but no lasting enjoyment to speak of. It makes me think of the U2 song, 'I Still Haven't Found What I'm Looking For.' The enemy wants to provide us with any other empty counterfeit at every turn. This is so we will never come to realize that the only thing that can permanently fill the void in our souls (created to hold the joy and pleasure of God) is time spent with Him.

From my personal encounters, I can say that this attribute is the one that has taken me most by surprise, especially as it has grown. When I first began to spend quiet time with God, I would certainly emerge feeling refreshed and comforted. However, as the relationship and communication has grown, I have begun to enjoy it more than I had ever thought

149

possible. I've had so much fun dancing in His presence and laughing at His, dare I say it, jokes. God is really entertaining and funny, especially when He says something that only you would get. Aren't inside jokes always the best kind? If these ideas are a reach, I understand because I have been there.

Let's pause and take a moment to open our hearts to what the Bible says about joy, rather than what the religious norm has taught us to accept. Let's return to Ecclesiastes 2, which reveals that the wisest man to ever live also understood that enJOYment alone comes from God, rather than the things he had been chasing all his life.

[See Ecclesiastes 2:24b-25 - This also, I saw, is from the hand of God, for apart from him who can eat or who can have enjoyment?]

It is generally thought that Solomon wrote this book in the latter part of his life, as opposed to Proverbs which he wrote earlier. Now the book of Proverbs has immense wisdom to be sure, but there is something to be said for learning from those who have lived it over the span of their life. We should choose to stand on the shoulders of this brilliant man and take to heart what he found to be true in his old age.

If that weren't enough, here is one more portion of Scripture that clearly reveals God's esteem for joy.

[See Nehemiah 8:9-12 - And Nehemiah, who was the governor, and Ezra the priest and scribe, and the Levites who taught the people said to all the people, "This day is holy to the LORD your God; do not mourn or weep." For all the people wept as they heard the words of the Law. Then he said to them, "Go your way. Eat the fat and drink sweet wine and send portions to anyone who has nothing ready, for this day is holy to our Lord. And do not be grieved, for the joy of the LORD is your strength." So the Levites calmed all the people, saying, "Be quiet, for this day is holy; do not be grieved." And all the people went their way to eat and drink and to send portions and to make great rejoicing, because they had understood the words that were declared to them.]

Now don't get me wrong, I am fully aware that there are sober times to be had with God. But I believe we tend to err on the side of seriousness rather than joy which causes us to miss out on a huge part of God's character by doing so. In these verses, the people were instructed to eat, drink, rejoice, and not be grieved for the joy of the Lord was their strength. Notice it does not say that the somberness of God would empower them! He was telling them to party. Whoever said that this word has to equate to debauchery and sin? God throws the absolute best party around and even calls it holy as we see here. I believe this illustrates that our default position should always be one of joy, because His is.

I can't leave this section without briefly discussing joy's comparison to a spring, or a fountain of fresh water. This attribute of God's is the source for newness that we all need to partake of on a regular basis. Naturally, I think of our kids and how they love to play in any kind of water. There is particular delight though when they find a bubbling, spraying, unpredictable play spot. This kind of water surges with new life and beckons us into adventure. I'm lining up first for a download of this in a spiritual sense! So while God's peace may be the vehicle that is consistently and powerfully pushing us forward, His joy is the means by which we access a bubbling up of new, energetic, and refreshing encounters.

[See Isaiah 12:3 (AMP) - Therefore with joy you will draw water from the springs of salvation.]

Disconnection Point

If we think about the link between these two attributes of peace and joy, I am struck with the idea that they are both emotions that people seek out of escapism. Whether it is through the use of cheap entertainment or maybe even a controlled substance, people are frantically trying to tap into peace and joy. This is because when we experience these two feelings, we are able to disconnect from the cares of life. Deep down we all know that we are not meant to live in this brokenness. Hence believers and unbelievers alike spend enormous amounts of time and money to unplug and experience a different reality, even if it is only momentary.

The exceptional part of this point is that now we know where lasting peace and joy is found. It is not in prime time television, any drink or drug, a new relationship, a long vacation, or the next big purchase. We were made for another reality – His reality in the kingdom of heaven. Plugging in to the peace and joy of God, in all of their fullness, will meet this same objective of disconnecting from the cares of the world. Might I add that it will not have any of the negative side effects of the other behaviors either!

As I surveyed the title of the chapter this week, I had the assumption that this would be a kicked back, easygoing time...hardly. These are not the lightweight things of the Bible. They are mighty weapons, and we need to regard them as such. God's attributes of peace and joy should not be simple components of our lives. Instead, they should perhaps be so prominently displayed that they become attractively contagious to others as well.

Week 8 Reflections & Meditations

Reflect: Can you remember a time of both peace and production? Or has every high output period of your life been related to high pressure? Recall a season filled with pleasure in your past. If it wasn't outright sinful (or in violation of God's best plan), what would prevent you from classifying that time as holy?

Meditate: Glance through the Week 8 Scriptures and pick several to meditate on this week. Write them in the space below, make a notecard, or create a memo on your phone to keep them handy. Writing them helps, speaking them helps, and praying them to God helps most of all.

Apply: When tempted toward pursuing escapism this week, why not try spending some fun time with God rather than your usual methods of entertainment, food, etc. Approach him as you would a dear friend. Don't make it religious! Journal the details below.

Week 8 Scripture Listing

Peaceful

-Numbers 6:24-26 - The LORD bless you and keep you; the LORD make his face to shine upon you and be gracious to you; the LORD lift up his countenance upon you and give you peace.

-Psalm 4:8 - In peace I will both lie down and sleep; for you alone, O LORD, make me dwell in safety.

-Isaiah 26:3-4 – You keep him in perfect peace whose mind is stayed on you, because he trusts in you. Trust in the LORD forever, for the LORD GOD is an everlasting rock.

-Isaiah 53:5 - But he was pierced for our transgressions; he was crushed for our iniquities; upon him was the chastisement that brought us peace, and with his wounds we are healed.

-Jeremiah 6:16 - Thus says the LORD: Stand by the roads, and look, and ask for the ancient paths, where the good way is; and walk in it, and find rest for your souls.

-John 14:27 - Peace I leave with you; my peace I give to you. Not as the world gives do I give to you. Let not your hearts be troubled, neither let them be afraid.

-John 16:33 - I have said these things to you, that in me you may have peace. In the world you will have tribulation. But take heart; I have overcome the world.

-Romans 8:6 - For to set the mind on the flesh is death, but to set the mind on the Spirit is life and peace.

Joyful

-Psalm 5:11 - But let all who take refuge in you rejoice; let them ever sing for joy, and spread your protection over them, that those who love your name may exult in you.

-Psalm 16:11 - You make known to me the path of life; in your presence there is fullness of joy; at your right hand are pleasures forevermore.

-Psalm 21:1-7 - O LORD, in your strength the king rejoices, and in your salvation how greatly he exults! You have given him his heart's desire and have not withheld the request of his lips. For you meet him with rich blessings; you set a crown of fine gold upon his head. He asked life of you; you gave it to him, length of days forever and ever. His glory is great through your salvation; splendor and majesty you bestow on him. For you make him most blessed forever; you make him glad with the joy of your presence. For the king trusts in the LORD, and through the steadfast love of the Most High he shall not be moved.

-Psalm 65:11-13 - You crown the year with your bounty; your wagon tracks overflow with abundance. The pastures of the wilderness overflow, the hills gird themselves with joy, the meadows clothe themselves with flocks, the valleys deck themselves with grain, they shout and sing together for joy.

-Jeremiah 15:16 - Your words were found, and I ate them, and your words became to me a joy and the delight of my heart, for I am called by your name, O LORD, God of hosts.

-John 15:11 - These things I have spoken to you, that my joy may be in you, and that your joy may be full.

-Philippians 2:13 – For it is God who works in you, both to will and to work for his good pleasure.

-Hebrews 12:1-2 - Therefore, since we are surrounded by so great a cloud of witnesses, let us also lay aside every weight, and sin which clings so closely, and let us run with endurance the race that is set before us, looking to Jesus, the founder and perfecter of our faith, who for the joy that was set before him endured the cross, despising the shame, and is seated at the right hand of the throne of God.

Disconnect

-Isaiah 55:12 - For you shall go out in joy and be led forth in peace; the mountains and the hills before you shall break forth into singing, and all the trees of the field shall clap their hands.

-Romans 14:17 - For the kingdom of God is not a matter of eating and drinking but of righteousness and peace and joy in the Holy Spirit.

-Romans 15:13 - May the God of hope fill you with all joy and peace in believing, so that by the power of the Holy Spirit you may abound in hope.

-Philippians 4:4-7 - Rejoice in the Lord always; again I will say, rejoice. Let your reasonableness be known to everyone. The Lord is at hand; do not be anxious about anything, but in everything by prayer and supplication with thanksgiving let your requests be made known to God. And the peace of God, which surpasses all understanding, will guard your hearts and your minds in Christ Jesus.

Week 9 – Jealous & Patient

I sincerely hope that your experience thus far has reaped enormous dividends in your relationship with God. That is what we need after all. This venture is not about acquiring book knowledge or pursuing growth for growth's sake. Sometimes I think that we may have the wrong idea that maturing spiritually is a destination or arrival to be sought after. If that were the case, I imagine life might be quite dull in the window of eternity! When in actuality, we are not meant to settle permanently anywhere. Instead, we are on a never ending adventure of growing relationally with the God of the universe.

If that path does not seem very exciting to you, try this scenario. Say you give a child a beautifully wrapped gift. How ecstatic are they as they stare at the completely wrapped present? What about when the wrapping is off, and they can see the new play thing that awaits? What about when the outer box is off, and they can admire all of the additional features and accessories? What about as you pull off all of the tape, metal ties, jaws of life holding the toy in the box? In my limited experience, the pleasure grows as the child sees the fullness of the present revealed.

We have the opportunity to be in a limitless relationship with God that plays out in this same escalating way, and it can happen even while we are here on earth. We just have to make the individual choice to take God out of the box and mentally release all of the limitations and preconceptions that keep Him tied down.

Much of the time, we leave God in the pretty package that attracted us to Him, and there He sits. God is not going to impose the gift of Himself on us, as much as He would like to. This segues right into our next attributes. The jealousy and patience of God may not make most top ten lists of His characteristics, but I propose they should as they take His love and value for each of us to a whole new level.

The One

Jealousy is described as vigilant in guarding a possession, hostile toward rivals, protective. While most of the time we may intellectually consider jealousy to be a negative emotion, I know that I can secretly appreciate when someone feels this way about me. Somehow I do not think I am alone in this either. Why do we react this way? Because if someone is jealous, it indicates that they want all of you to themselves. It speaks to your importance and significance in their eyes.

In human interactions, the available supply of love and affection is limited. This is ultimately what creates jealousy: when the draws on a person exceed their capacity, and people have to cope with getting less than they prefer of that particular person. Now obviously we do not have to be jealous of God. There is absolutely enough of Him to go around. But on our end, is it outside the realm of comprehension that God would be jealous for us because He is getting less than He would prefer?

Imagine, every person that He created is incredibly special to Him, and we all have a distinctly individual way of loving Him in return. This brings us to the point that regardless of the number of believers that will ever come into the Kingdom, God still remains jealous for the one.

[See Matthew 18:12-13 – What do you think? If a man has a hundred sheep, and one of them has gone astray, does he not leave the ninety-nine on the mountains and go in search of the one that went astray? And if he finds it, truly, I say to you, he rejoices over it more than over the ninety-nine that never went astray.]

Can we even begin to wrap our brains around this? The Being that spoke the complexities of life into order, sees and receives something extraordinary from each of us that cannot be duplicated. Because of this, He does become vigilant and protective when our love and affection begin to get dwindled away on other things.

Intimacy is very expensive to build, and we only have room for so many of these costly relationships. God wants to be at the very top of our lists. This should absolutely transform the notion of our individual worth in His eyes. I have the impression that humanity in general thinks that God could simply take them or leave them, as if they are merely an option in His eyes. We tend to think we are just not that special, when that is actually the farthest thing from the truth.

Even as we make progress toward applying this emotion to the God of all creation, I also don't think we understand its appropriate outworking in any relationship. For an illustration, let me share a brief story about my husband and me. When Austen and I first met at Texas A&M (Whoop!), I was a freshman and he was a sophomore. While we were both interested in dating one another, since I was younger and new to campus, I told him I did not want to be exclusive yet. He put up with this for just a few weeks before letting me know that this was simply not working for him! At the time, I was a bit offended that he would opt to have none of me if he couldn't have it all.

As I was reflecting this week, I realized that this is God's posture of jealousy toward us as well. Notice, that my now husband did not stalk me on other dates or turn into a psychopath, which is often how we may picture jealousy. Rather, he kindly but firmly withdrew from the relationship until I later came to my senses. Does this sound more like the loving and good God that we are coming to know? Oh yes, God can be hostile as a result of His jealousy. However, this hostility is not directed at the objects of His affection, but instead, at His rivals.

[See Ezekiel 36:6-7 - Therefore prophesy concerning the land of Israel, and say to the mountains and hills, to the ravines and valleys, Thus says the Lord GOD: Behold, I have spoken in my jealous wrath, because you have suffered the reproach of the nations. Therefore thus says the Lord GOD: I swear that the nations that are all around you shall themselves suffer reproach.]

God will certainly do everything in His power to weaken and disarm all opponents. In fact, He goes beyond that. Scripture says that He openly shamed the powers of darkness in His triumph at the cross. Can you imagine that in the context of a human love story?

[See Colossians 2:13-15 - And you, who were dead in your trespasses and the uncircumcision of your flesh, God made alive together with him, having forgiven us all our trespasses, by canceling the record of debt that stood against us with its legal demands. This he set aside, nailing it to the cross. He disarmed the rulers and authorities and put them to open shame, by triumphing over them in him.]

Yet, even with God having done all of this in His watchfulness over us, the decision to enter into exclusive relationship is still ultimately ours. So this is what the healthy jealousy of God looks like: vigilant over and longing for the one, passionately hostile toward any rivals, and respectfully firm while awaiting our decision.

Stood Up

The Bible has much to say about the patience of God, which is characterized as the capacity to accept or tolerate delay, trouble, or suffering without getting angry or upset. Although in many Scripture translations, this attribute is referred to as His longsuffering. It may be tough for us to think of a perfect and complete God as having suffering, but He does and it is a direct result of the free will that He gave us (in combination with His extraordinary patience). It is a painful thing for Him to watch us being destroyed by the enemy; and He has been doing it for a very long time, at least according to our stopwatch.

[See 2 Peter 3:8-9 - But do not overlook this one fact, beloved, that with the Lord one day is as a thousand years, and a thousand years as one day. The Lord is not slow to fulfill his promise as some count slowness, but is patient toward you, not wishing that any should perish, but that all should reach repentance.]

As we try to grasp the immensity of the patience that is God's very nature, my mind wanders toward the idea of being 'stood up' in a human context. We most often think of this situation as a hazard of dating. However, it can happen in all spheres of life, from asking guests to your home as an adult to inviting friends to your birthday party as a child. There is not much that can make you feel more unmotivated to keep putting yourself out there, as when the people you have opened yourself up to do not even show up.

Picture the embarrassment on a single's face alone in a restaurant or the crestfallen look of a child as their hopes are dashed. There is no doubt pain here and much of it. When these situations happen to us, the enemy goes to work double time, whispering in our ears and 'helping' interpret these situations to wound us in far greater ways. God does not give a second look at the enemy's lying lips, but He still does feel the sting.

Suppose for a moment, there is a beautiful banquet being prepared on a daily basis. The food has been cooked, the drinks have been poured, the place settings have been arranged, the lighting is just right – and then the whole production is at a standstill while waiting for the invited guests to arrive. The time passes and no one comes. So the arrangements are cleaned up, much of the provisions going straight into the garbage, only to have the whole thing recreated the following day.

If the host were a human, you can guarantee that they would only put this on a few times before resigning themselves to the fact that no one would be attending! And here again, God continues to defy our status quo. With great patience, He sets up the banqueting table day in and day out in the hopes that all of His treasured children will accept the invitation and come running to the feast.

[See Psalm 23:5-6 - You prepare a table before me in the presence of my enemies; you anoint my head with oil; my cup overflows. Surely goodness and mercy shall follow me all the days of my life, and I shall dwell in the house of the LORD forever.]

Even as God is stood up time after time, His patience and longsuffering endure the pain, because His will is for everyone to have a chance to enter into the Kingdom of Heaven (again see 2 Peter 3). I am awestruck by the fortitude that such behavior requires, while simultaneously being nauseated at the waste that is occurring. You see, I consider it waste, because I have limited understanding in a limited world. For God, it is not waste at all, because His supply is infinite. He can overflow every created being's cup of needs every day for eternity and still never get tapped out.

Entitlement Issues

One thing that has been noted about the current generation reaching adulthood (yes, I'm speaking of the millenials) is that they have 'entitlement issues.' Entitlement is the guarantee of having access to something. This mindset is sickening to people who were raised in a previous generation, because they have had to work so hard for what they have. The difficulty of functioning in this contrast is understandable, but these old mindsets are part of the poison that the enemy has used to continually infiltrate our hearts. They certainly have made a mentality of being saved by good works much easier to come by.

Instead of getting annoyed at the cheekiness of the younger people, I believe that God wants us to embrace their attitude so that it may be imparted to everyone. He has been building generation upon generation in the people of faith to get to a group who would be bold enough to believe that they have full access to Him and His Kingdom. So maybe, we need all believers to come to a place of having some entitlement issues!

[See Isaiah 41:4 - Who has performed and done this, calling the generations from the beginning? I, the LORD, the first, and with the last; I am he.]

This necessary core value of knowing we are guaranteed access to God's unlimited supply will come out of comprehending our worth and standing with Him. Confidence in our position will be further solidified by beholding His jealousy and patience for each of us. We must see our God as One who is passionately and permanently jealous for us and who patiently remains the gracious host always prepared with a waiting, overflowing banquet table of provision for the seeking ones.

[See Psalm 42:7-8 - Deep calls to deep at the roar of your waterfalls; all your breakers and your waves have gone over me. By day the LORD commands his steadfast love, and at night his song is with me, a prayer to the God of my life.]

Week 9 Reflections & Meditations

Reflect: Recall a time in your history when you were overwhelmed with feelings of jealousy. Were you able to calmly stand by as your needs (or preferences) were unmet? What would have driven you to wait it out, to patiently suffer those feelings and wait for them to turn their affections toward you?

Meditate: Glance through the Week 9 Scriptures and pick several to meditate on this week. Write them in the space below, make a notecard, or create a memo on your phone to keep them handy. Writing them helps, speaking them helps, and praying them to God helps most of all.

Apply: What is your gut check response to the thought that to God, you are The One? Or the thought that He is constantly providing a banqueting table with everything you need, whether you partake or not? What would it look like to operate with an awareness of His jealousy and patience every day? Journal the details below.

Week 9 Scripture Listing

Jealous

-Exodus 34:14 - For you shall worship no other god, for the LORD, whose name is Jealous, is a jealous God.

-Deuteronomy 4:24 - For the LORD your God is a consuming fire, a jealous God.

-Psalm 78:58 - For they provoked him to anger with their high places; they moved him to jealousy with their idols.

-Proverbs 27:4 - Wrath is cruel, anger is overwhelming, but who can stand before jealousy?

-Song of Solomon 8:6-7 - Set me as a seal upon your heart, as a seal upon your arm, for love is strong as death, jealousy is fierce as the grave. Its flashes are flashes of fire, the very flame of the LORD. Many waters cannot quench love, neither can floods drown it.

-Zechariah 8:1-2 - And the word of the LORD of hosts came, saying, Thus says the LORD of hosts: I am jealous for Zion with great jealousy, and I am jealous for her with great wrath.

-2 Corinthians 11:2-3 - For I feel a divine jealousy for you, since I betrothed you to one husband, to present you as a pure virgin to Christ. But I am afraid that as the serpent deceived Eve by his cunning, your thoughts will be led astray from a sincere and pure devotion to Christ.

-James 4:4-8 - You adulterous people! Do you not know that friendship with the world is enmity with God? Therefore whoever wishes to be a friend of the world makes himself an enemy of God. Or do you suppose it is to no purpose that the Scripture says, "He yearns jealously over the spirit that he has made to dwell in us"? But he gives more grace. Therefore it says, "God opposes the proud, but gives grace to the humble." Submit yourselves therefore to God. Resist the devil, and he will flee from you. Draw near to God, and he will draw near to you. Cleanse your hands, you sinners, and purify your hearts, you double-minded.

Patient

-Exodus 34:5-6 - The LORD descended in the cloud and stood with him there, and proclaimed the name of the LORD. The LORD passed before him and proclaimed, "The LORD, the LORD, a God merciful and gracious, slow to anger, and abounding in steadfast love and faithfulness."

-Psalm 86:15 - But you, O Lord, are a God merciful and gracious, slow to anger and abounding in steadfast love and faithfulness.

-Romans 2:4 - Or do you presume on the riches of his kindness and forbearance and patience, not knowing that God's kindness is meant to lead you to repentance?

-1 Corinthians 13:4-8 - Love is patient and kind; love does not envy or boast; it is not arrogant or rude. It does not insist on its own way; it is not irritable or resentful; it does not rejoice at wrongdoing, but rejoices with the truth. Love bears all things, believes all things, hopes all things, endures all things. Love never ends.

-Galatians 5:22-25 - But the fruit of the Spirit is love, joy, peace, patience, kindness, goodness, faithfulness, gentleness, self-control; against such things there is no law. And those who belong to Christ Jesus have crucified the flesh with its passions and desires. If we live by the Spirit, let us also keep in step with the Spirit.

-Colossians 3:12-13 - Put on then, as God's chosen ones, holy and beloved, compassionate hearts, kindness, humility, meekness, and patience, bearing with one another and, if one has a complaint against another, forgiving each other; as the Lord has forgiven you, so you also must forgive.

-1 Timothy 1:15-17 - The saying is trustworthy and deserving of full acceptance, that Christ Jesus came into the world to save sinners, of whom I am the foremost. But I received mercy for this reason, that in me, as the foremost, Jesus Christ might display his perfect patience as an example to those who were to believe in him for eternal life. To the King of the ages, immortal, invisible, the only God, be honor and glory forever and ever. Amen.

Week 10 - Personal

This week we head out on one last exploratory mission into the heart of God. The message that I feel so compelled to leave us with is that of His nature as a uniquely personal God. I believe it is one final misunderstanding that needs to be combated in all of our hearts and minds as we seek to know Him more deeply. Personal is characterized as concerning one's private life, relationships, and emotions, rather than matters connected with one's public or professional career.

When we think about the concept of privacy, there is the idea of some sort of barrier put up to keep out the intrusion of others. Typically, there are some people in all of our lives who are allowed beyond the barriers to come to know us as we really are. So now I must ask, is God counted among them? Or do we choose to keep Him at a distance, hoping that He will like our public persona and come no further?

This image of a personal God may seem exciting in one sense to have someone know us so intimately, but it may also be a bit unnerving to think of allowing Him to get that close. Sometimes, it actually feels safer to remain lost in the proverbial crowd, which is exactly where the enemy would like for us to stay.

The Comparison Trap

One primary way that we limit how personal our relationship with God becomes is by being too concerned with what other people are doing or thinking. After all, it is not necessarily the most common thing in the world to chase after an unseen God with reckless abandon, which is exactly what I am advocating here. So if you do begin to look around for other sojourners, they may be hard to find. It is far easier for most people to remain detached from God in neutral, or worse, cynical mode.

Whether we are seasoned believers that choose to stay at 'safe' distances from God because of things we have observed or whether we are those who absolutely refuse to come to faith because of this hypocrite or that unfair situation, it really is all the same thing. We are too busy looking around instead of looking up. We are consumed with comparisons and are letting the misunderstandings of others cloud our own opinion of God, when we have enough trouble already with our own individual lies from the enemy. If we have difficulty refuting the handful of lies aimed straight at our hearts, we are going to have tremendous struggles with the mountain of lies that have been tailor made for others.

In the end, it will be a very solo you and I standing in front of the throne of the God of the cosmos. Nothing anyone else said or did will matter in that moment. So what do others' opinions and experiences have to do with each of us and a relationship with a personal God who came from heaven to earth to save?

He is the one who sent His son, Jesus, as a sacrifice to mend the relationship, forever tearing down the curtain of legalism and religion in the name of freedom and relationship. This is the God that is worth forgetting all about others (and the comparison trap) and diving headlong into the quest for His heart.

Access Granted?

If we can hurdle the obstacle that is the distraction of others' lives, we then come face-to-face with the decision of whether or not to grant God full access. Of course, He does know all anyway; but it is up to us whether we are going to engage on our end. I liken it to news coverage. It is one thing for Him to read the daily headlines from afar. It is quite another for Him to be able to hear us give our first hand, personalized, even animated accounts. The entire counsel of Scripture points to the fact that this is what He wants – an ongoing dialogue, a connection to our very hearts.

The passage quoted below is interesting, in that, it has often been taught from the perspective of Jesus seeking entrance with those who have not yet come to believe.

[See Revelation 3:20-21 - Behold, I stand at the door and knock. If anyone hears my voice and opens the door, I will come in to him and eat with him, and he with me. The one who conquers, I will grant him to sit with me on my throne, as I also conquered and sat down with my Father on his throne.]

In actuality, these words are addressing one of the seven churches taught about in this book of the Bible (church, as in a group of people who have already believed). This is important, because it shows that there is a definite contrast between people who have simply believed and those who have granted God full access to their hearts. Beyond the sheer enjoyment that a highly personal relationship provides, why is this distinction significant? When we read the second verse, we see that giving Him access is a key to conquering - intimacy will lead to ultimate victory.

Jesus stands before each of our doors, waiting to be let in, making His request known by the sound of a knock, but never imposing. Sometimes, I think we wonder why God does not demand that we open the door. We have difficulty making the decisions and taking the steps that this personal God desires, so we wish that He would just do it for us. I firmly believe that no one would love a God like that.

Imagine the typical nosy neighbor or aggressive journalist. Do we ever want to give such people true views into our lives? No, there is always strong push back in these situations. The only way that this venture is going to live up to its potential is by us boldly choosing to open the door. He will be there ready; just try it and see.

Finally Understood

It will take courage and fortitude to complete this journey with God, because we are being opposed with every step. Given this, we will need refueling along the way. Perhaps, finding the solace of finally being understood can serve as one of our pit stops. As humanity goes, we all have very different struggles. As such, it is quite easy for us to get wrong impressions about each other. God is the only One who can thoroughly understand our feelings, because He alone truly knows the path we traverse. It follows that He is the only One we can count on to never misunderstand us.

[See Psalm 56:8 (MSG) - You've kept track of my every toss and turn through the sleepless nights, each tear entered in your ledger, each ache written in your book.]

How deeply do these thoughts from the Psalms resonate with you? Toss, turn, sleepless, tear, ache. These are brutally honest terms that would not have been shared by someone who still had God beyond the barriers. They were penned by someone who had moved past the perceptions of others, taken the step of vulnerably allowing God complete access, and become utterly aware of what it means to be known and understood by a very personal God.

Finishing Touch

Yes, God is oh so personal. He has loved each one of us forever – before we were even a twinkle in our parents' eyes as the saying goes.

[See Psalm 139:16 - Your eyes saw my unformed substance; in your book were written, every one of

them, the days that were formed for me, when as yet there was none of them.]

God watched and waited throughout time: the meeting of our ancestors, our birth, our growth, our wanderings, until we finally reached the decision point of whether we would love Him in return. He has been focused on this moment through literal eons, and it is our astounding privilege to have it. Individually, we get to choose to love Him back or to turn our back.

If you have never made the decision to love this astonishingly good God back, let's put the finishing touch on this journey by doing so. And even if you have but still feel a fresh desire to pledge yourself to Him again, just speak this out along with me:

Father God - Thank you for creating me. Thank you for loving me. Thank you for saving me through the sacrifice of your son, Jesus. Thank you for forgiving all of my past, present, and future sins.

Today I lay down my own way of doing things. I turn from my willful independence. I choose to commit to loving and following you for all of my remaining days.

MISUNDERSTOOD

Lead me and teach me. Keep me close to your heart. Guard me from any misunderstandings as I seek to know You forevermore!

Week 10 Reflections & Meditations

Reflect: Have you noticed situations where your progress was limited, in either tangible ways or just in your thinking, due to making comparisons to those around you? Why do you think this trap is so hard to escape? Have you ever been in relationship with someone where you knew it was not safe to grant them full access to your life?

Meditate: Glance through the Week 10 Scriptures and pick several to meditate on this week. Write them in the space below, make a notecard, or create a memo on your phone to keep them handy. Writing them helps, speaking them helps, and praying them to God helps most of all.

Apply: Live this week with an awareness that the One who perfectly understands you is excitedly waiting for you to become aware of this fact and to capitalize on it. Enjoy and discuss even the minute details with Him. He is so personally interested in the happenings of your life. Journal the details below.

185

Week 10 Scripture Listing

-Genesis 1:31a - And God saw everything that he had made, and behold, it was very good.

-Psalm 139:1-3 - O LORD, you have searched me and known me! You know when I sit down and when I rise up; you discern my thoughts from afar. You search out my path and my lying down and are acquainted with all my ways.

-Jeremiah 1:4-5 - Now the word of the LORD came to me, saying, "Before I formed you in the womb I knew you, and before you were born I consecrated you; I appointed you a prophet to the nations."

-Matthew 6:31-33 - Therefore do not be anxious, saying, 'What shall we eat?' or 'What shall we drink?' or 'What shall we wear?' For the Gentiles seek after all these things, and your heavenly Father knows that you need them all. But seek first the kingdom of God and his righteousness, and all these things will be added to you.

-Luke 12:6-7 - Are not five sparrows sold for two pennies? And not one of them is forgotten before God. Why, even the hairs of your head are all numbered. Fear not; you are of more value than many sparrows.

-John 10:7-14 - So Jesus again said to them, "Truly, truly, I say to you, I am the door of the sheep. All who came before me are thieves and robbers, but the sheep did not listen to them. I am the door. If anyone enters by me, he will be saved and will go in and out and find pasture. The thief comes only to steal and kill and destroy. I came that they may have life and have it abundantly. I am the good shepherd. The good shepherd lays down his life for the sheep. He who is a hired hand and not a shepherd, who does not own the sheep, sees the wolf coming and leaves the sheep and flees, and the wolf snatches them and scatters them. He flees because he is a hired hand and cares nothing for the sheep. I am the good shepherd. I know my own and my own know me."

-John 21:21-22 - When Peter saw him, he said to Jesus, "Lord, what about this man?" Jesus said to him, "If it is my will that he remain until I come, what is that to you? You follow me!"

-Philippians 1:3-6 - I thank my God in all my remembrance of you, always in every prayer of mine for you all making my prayer with joy, because of your partnership in the gospel from the first day until now.

MISUNDERSTOOD

And I am sure of this, that he who began a good work in you will bring it to completion at the day of Jesus Christ.

Afterword - The Invitation Onward

In Ephesians 6, the Bible instructs us to put on the whole armor of God in order to wage war effectively in this battle of the ages against our adversary, satan.

[See Ephesians 6:10-18 - Finally, be strong in the Lord and in the strength of his might. Put on the whole armor of God, that you may be able to stand against the schemes of the devil. For we do not wrestle against flesh and blood, but against the rulers, against the authorities, against the cosmic powers over this present darkness, against the spiritual forces of evil in the heavenly places. Therefore take up the whole armor of God, that you may be able to withstand in the evil day, and having done all, to stand firm. Stand therefore, having fastened on the belt of truth, and having put on the breastplate of righteousness, and, as shoes for your feet, having put on the readiness given by the gospel of peace. In all circumstances take up the shield of faith, with which you can extinguish all the flaming darts of the evil one; and take the helmet of salvation, and the sword of the Spirit, which is the word of God, praying at all times in the Spirit, with all prayer and supplication. To that

end, keep   alert   with   all   perseverance,
making supplication for all the saints.]

The first piece of armor described in this critical passage is the belt of truth. Just as we refasten, loosen, or tighten natural belts as our bodies change, we must continue to spiritually adjust our 'belts' by seeking truth about the nature of God.

I believe that this has to be our starting point when we begin to feel weak on any given day or in any given battle – solidifying and believing the truth about His heart toward us. So please, for the sake of our army's onward march to victory, plan to revisit your journaling and notes here as often as necessary.

Also keep in mind, this text was never intended to be an end in and of itself. The book exploring the nature of God will never close. I am honored that this might occupy just a few pages in the story of the opening of God's heart to humanity. May this simply be your jumping off point, a sentence starter if you will, in your own personal exploration of God. He has so much He wants to say specifically to each of us. There can be no one-size, fits-all revelation, especially on this side of eternity.

To quote the great C.S. Lewis from the epic Chronicles of Narnia: 'All their life in this world and all their adventures had only been the cover and the title page: now at last they were beginning Chapter One of the Great Story which no one on earth has read: which goes on for ever: in which every chapter is better than the one before.'

MISUNDERSTOOD

a note from andrea -

Reviews are absolute gold to authors!
If you've enjoyed this book, would you consider
rating and reviewing it on www.Amazon.com?

thank you!

MISUNDERSTOOD

about the author

Andrea Joy Moede is a recovering over achiever who has traveled a long road of transformation. While she grew up in an amazing, believing family, she was ultimately left still searching for God. This was because she hadn't yet made the shift from dutiful religion to passionate relationship. As a young person, she set out to conquer the world with full scholarships to Texas A&M's business school and SMU's law school. When law school didn't quite fit the bill, she embarked on a career in accounting and finance at KPMG, Valero Energy, and USAA. She finally ended up spending time in an accounting PhD program at the University of Texas at San Antonio.

During this period, she was running from God and trying to determine her own destiny, before finally realizing that life on His path was so much better than anywhere else. She came to this understanding during the unexpectedly quiet years of being a young stay at home mom. She then began to listen to what God wanted to do with her life instead.

Now she is only determined to be a receiver of God's love and provision and to follow wherever He leads. She is excited about helping people come into the fullness of both their identity and calling and believes that this is best accomplished by beholding God in all of His fullness first.

When not writing, you can catch her busy with some of her favorite things - highly doctored coffee, endorphin inducing workouts, schmaltzy movies, long naps on rainy days, really good Italian food, coaching her kids sports teams, and sitting down with just about any book.

She lives in the Houston area with her husband – Austen, their two busy boys – Owen and Colsten, and their equally busy baby girl – Adelyn. They are active members of The Crossing Church in The Woodlands. When not enduring the climate of South Texas, they all prefer to escape to the mountains.